CORNELL
UNIVERSITY HOCKEY

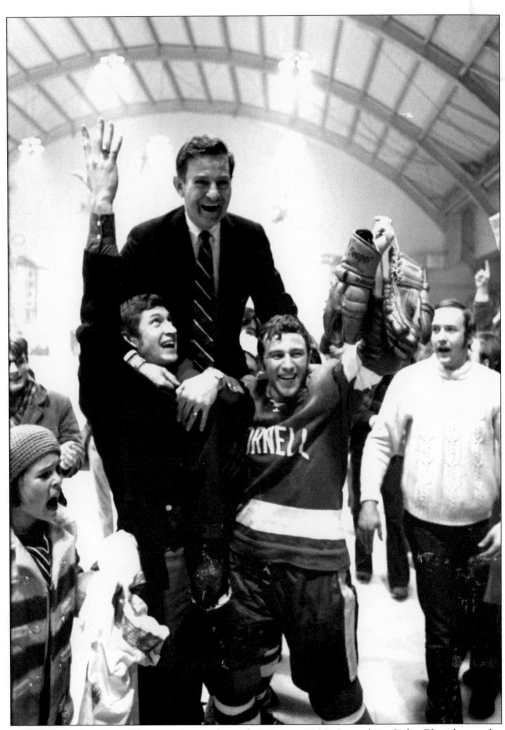

In 1970, the historic Olympic Arena (now known as 1932 Arena) in Lake Placid was the perfect setting for Cornell to complete the only perfect season of the modern NCAA Division I era. Ned Harkness, the coach who had sculpted a hockey dynasty, was carried off the ice, never to coach another Division I game again. (Cornell University Archives.)

CORNELL UNIVERSITY HOCKEY

Adam Wodon
with Research by Arthur Mintz

ARCADIA

First published 2004

Published by Arcadia Publishing,
Charleston SC, Chicago IL, Portsmouth NH, San Francisco CA

Printed in Great Britain

Library of Congress Catalog Card Number: 2004108611

For all general information, contact Arcadia Publishing:
Telephone 843-853-2070
Fax 843-853-0044
E-mail sales@arcadiapublishing.com
For customer service and orders:
Toll-free 1-888-313-2665

Visit us on the Internet at www.arcadiapublishing.com

For my first line: Marcy, Brett, and Cameron.

CONTENTS

ACKNOWLEDGMENTS

Thank you most of all to Arthur Mintz, who served as much more than a researcher. He was an editor, an ace go-fer, and a guide for the historical framework of the project. His contributions were wide-ranging and invaluable.

My gratitude goes to everyone at the Cornell University Archives for their patience, hard work, and hospitality. In particular, thanks to Laura Linke, Elaine Engst, Kari Smith, C. J. Lance-Duboscq, Rhea Garen, and Bryan Vliet. I am similarly grateful to everyone at the Cornell Athletic Communications office for their patience and assistance, including Laura Stange, Elli Harkness, and Marlene Crockford, as well as those at the hockey office, including Sue Detzer and coach Mike Schafer.

The *Cornell Daily Sun* provided many of the photographs and access to the office. Thank you, in particular, to Christine Papio and Shalini Saxena. Likewise, at the *Ithaca Journal*, I thank Bruce Estes, Tom Fleischman, and Simon Wheeler. The following photographers graciously contributed their work: Larry Baum, Jeff Wang, Pedro Cancel, Tim McKinney, Adriano Manocchia, Nancie Battaglia, and many others from the past.

Thanks to all the past research I leaned upon, in particular Neil Fidelman's authoritative history of Cornell hockey, a special section that ran in the *Cornell Daily Sun* in 1982; the work of Arthur Kaminsky and Howie Borkan; *Good Sports: A History of Cornell Athletics* by Robert J. Kane; *Cornell Football 1949–1976 from Home Game Programs* edited by Ben Mintz; and various *Ithaca Journal* and *Daily Sun* writers.

And special thanks go to those who took the time to talk or help out in their own way: Neil Cohen, Bill Mack, John Hughes, Steve Hagwell, Mike Teeter, Murray Deathe, Dave Cutting, Laing Kennedy, Peter Shier, Darren Eliot, and Brock Tredway.

INTRODUCTION

Sports is nothing without its history. The past serves as a guidepost by which we compare the current era, and it is often the background by which we remember our own lives. History and tradition are things that can show us a way to the future, things we can draw from for a sense of community.

Of course, it helps when the history is successful, as with Cornell Big Red hockey. But success is often perpetuated because history is embraced. How a community treats its past says a lot about how much it appreciates what it has now, and where it is going. Every person who makes up the Big Red hockey experience cherishes their part in history, and nods to it in their own way.

The coaches are members of a unique club, of which there have been just six members in nearly 50 years. Each one has gone on to other successes and failures, but all have treated their job as something to cherish in and of itself, and not merely as a stepping stone.

The players, most of whom know little about Cornell hockey history upon their arrival, quickly learn. They work together to polish the trophies won by those who have gone before them, they study the way in which past championship teams were built and the hurdles they surpassed along the way, and they learn the names and backgrounds of the players who wore their numbers before them.

"As soon as I took No. 25, coach was like, 'As soon as you go on the ice, people are going to see No. 25 and think Joe Nieuwendyk,' and I know that," said Sam Paolini, who played from 1999 to 2003. "It's unbelievable the players that come out of here and the players we have. And I think all the players realize that, because before every game, Coach Schafer instills it in us— 'Play for your school, play for the fans, play for yourself.'"

But it does not end there.

The spirited pep band is ever-aware of living up to its importance. Ask members how a song got started or how it evolved, and they can tell you the legend.

The home crowd—a.k.a. the Lynah Faithful—is perhaps the most essential part of the Cornell hockey experience. Being a member of the Faithful means not just passionately exhorting every cheer in perfect unison at the perfect time of the game, for years and years and years; it also means knowing how these cheers came to be, even down to the names of the people who started them.

The call of history even strikes the public-address announcers and broadcasters, who can reel off the names of those who have gone before them, appreciative of the opportunity to be in their company.

Hopefully, the tradition of Cornell hockey is sufficiently captured within these pages. Assuredly, there are many stories that remain untold, either because a photograph does not exist or because space does not allow for elaboration. Nonetheless, it is still true that a picture says a thousand words, and as a result, this book tells a lot. The beauty, of course, is that more chapters remain to be written.

My first encounter with Big Red hockey came as a freshman at Ithaca College in 1988. My knowledge of college hockey was merely tangential, thanks to whatever I could glean from the *Hockey News* at that time. But I knew enough, and loved hockey enough, to know that covering Cornell was something I was very interested in as a new member of WICB, the Ithaca College student radio station.

It took all of about five minutes to figure out what was special. From the moment I nearly jumped out of my skin as the fans yelled "Red!" during the national anthem, until the final, frenzied moments of a home-team win, I was enraptured by the sights, the sounds, and the passion of Cornell hockey.

In the years since that first experience, I have worked in and seen all levels of sports, from rinks in beat-up mill towns, to arenas in new cities popping up out of cornfields, to multi-purpose entertainment palaces in big cities trying to keep up with the times.

But one place keeps drawing me back. In an era of corporate ownership, seat licenses, stadium-naming rights, canned music, wandering huckster emcees, third jerseys, and glowing pucks . . . Cornell hockey remains the essence of sport.

—Adam Wodon

"The fans give us so much energy. As soon as we make a good play, and they start cheering, we feed off them. And it's unbelievable how much noise they can generate."—Sam Paolini, team member from 1999 to 2003. (Cornell University Archives.)

One

BEEBE LAKE

THE EARLY YEARS

Long before there was a Lynah Faithful, long before there was a Frozen Four, when the names Ken Dryden, Ned Harkness, and Joe Nieuwendyk were but a distant glimmer, before in fact there was an Eastern College Athletic Conference (ECAC), Ivy League, or even a National Collegiate Athletic Association (NCAA), there existed intercollegiate ice hockey. First played by Yale and Johns Hopkins in 1896, intercollegiate matches soon included several of the more esteemed institutions in the East.

In general, this action took place in and around the big cities along the East Coast, at places like Yale, Harvard, Columbia, and Princeton. Meanwhile, in the far reaches of upstate New York, a Cornell professor helped raise funds to build a rink on Beebe Lake, in the middle of Cornell's campus, though it was not until 1901 that students at Cornell finally got organized. It was then that G. A. Smith arranged a series of three games, all to take place in the Philadelphia area during one week. The tour was a success, with Cornell winning all three contests, against Swarthmore, Penn, and Princeton.

Cornell's group was unable to get any competition the next season, mainly because of the distance from New York City, where many games were played. The club then resumed play in 1902–03 with a pair of games, a win over Princeton and a loss to Yale. The organizers of the hockey club ran into a series of confrontations with the Cornell administration, however, and were not officially recognized for three years. The boiling point came when a player who had been expelled from the school tried to compete under a false name. The faculty got wind of it and disbanded the team.

After several stops and starts, finally, in 1906, Ralph Lally convinced school officials to sponsor the team once again. "Hockey practice today," announced the *Cornell Daily Sun*. "Providing that it does not thaw, all candidates for the hockey team are requested to report at Beebe Lake this afternoon." With that, Cornell played its first home game, a 7-0 win over Rochester on Beebe Lake. A perfect four-game record the next year included two more games on Beebe Lake, the last matches that would take place there until the 1913–14 season.

In the early 1900s, the East Coast schools managed to form college hockey's first true conference, the Intercollegiate League. But despite repeated attempts to gain entrance into the group, Cornell was denied. The university was also still wary of allowing the team to play games anywhere but on school grounds. That restriction was lifted in 1908, and Cornell opened the season with three games against Penn at a new city rink in Cleveland. Finally, the team gained the services of Talbot Hunter as coach in 1909, lending an air of legitimacy that helped Cornell gain entrance into the league.

During its second year in the league, 1910–11, Cornell stunned the hockey world—what little of it there was—by compiling a perfect 10-0 record, while playing 10 road games, to capture the Intercollegiate League championship. It would be Cornell's last championship of any kind for more than 50 years.

Things slid downhill from there, including an 0-7 season in 1912–13, which included three straight losses to Princeton at Syracuse opening the year. Cornell was outscored 17-5 in the games, as the Tigers, led by the greatest player of his time, Hobey Baker, dominated.

By 1916, the Intercollegiate League had disbanded due to financial problems and the looming World War I. Shortly thereafter, Cornell's hockey program folded as well. It was not until 1920 that the program was restarted, when Nicholas Bawlf, a former professional player, came to Ithaca. Over his next 27 years as head coach, Bawlf was able to institute a regular schedule of games, both home and away. The problem was that many of those games, especially at home, were not even played. Other schools were building enclosed facilities, but Cornell's fortunes were still subject to the whims of Ithaca weather. Beebe Lake did not always freeze enough, and in some years, whole seasons had to be cancelled. When Cornell did play, it was often with little actual practice time.

Following an 0-4 season in 1946–47, in which Cornell lost by a combined score of 38-5, Bawlf passed away. Assistant coach Arthur Boehringer held things together for one more year, but after another 0-4 season (and a 43-3 scoring discrepancy), Cornell shut down the program. Too many other schools had rinks with artificial (man-made) ice and quality practice time, putting Cornell at a major disadvantage. Supporters of hockey in town focused their efforts on raising money for a new indoor facility on Cornell's campus. For years, those efforts were fruitless.

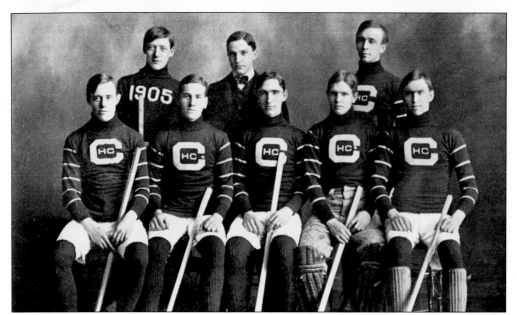

G. A. Smith, a graduate student, organized a group of freshmen and sophomores in March 1900 for an intrasquad scrimmage, but could not plan games with other schools because of the $100 entry fee to the Intercollegiate League. The next year, the Cornell group did organize three intercollegiate games. The school's first hockey team, seen here in 1902, included, from left to right, the following: (first row) J. M. Lee, R. C. Armstrong, captain H. M. Wood, C. H. Day, and I. C. Dederer; (second row) Philip Lewis, manager H. M. Ferguson, and A. R. Ellis. (*Cornellian.*)

Talbot Hunter (center), previously stationed at the University of Toronto, coached Cornell in two stints, 1909–1912 and 1914–1916, for a total of five years. He was the first full-time hockey coach, and led the soccer team as well. Captain and goalie Bill Matchneer stands at right, with Edmund "Stub" Magner at left, in this photograph from the 1910–11 Intercollegiate League championship season. (*Cornellian.*)

11

Nicky Bawlf trains his team on Beebe Lake. In those days, it was said that if you were willing to clear snow off the lake at any time day or night, you were on the team. (Cornell University Archives.)

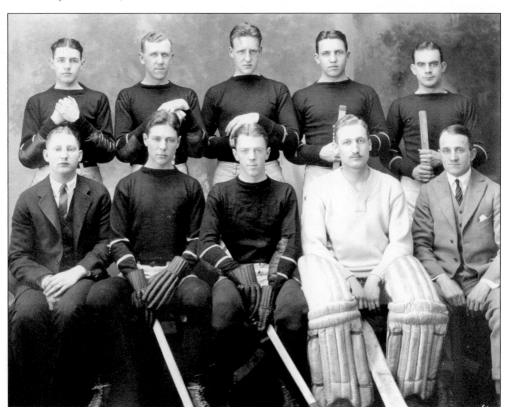

Members of the 1922 squad are, from left to right, as follows: (first row) Albert Crockin (manager), John Brockway, George Thornton (captain), Stanley Wight, and Nicholas Bawlf (coach); (second row) Charles MacDonald, William Goetz, John Ogden, Charles Davidson, and Caesar Grasselli. (Cornell University Archives.)

Cornell hockey went on hiatus when a lack of funds and an impending World War I led to the dissolution of the Intercollegiate League. The Cornell program returned in 1920 under new coach Nicholas Bawlf. In its first game of the new era, Cornell lost to Hamilton 2-0, on Beebe Lake, on January 15, 1921. The *Ithaca Journal* wrote, "The playing of the Ithacans . . . showed great promise and was of high character, despite the fact that the squad had had but a week's practice previous to the game." Following this season, college hockey switched to six players on the ice per side instead of seven, with three periods instead of two halves. Players rarely substituted throughout the course of the game. (Cornell University Archives.)

A game is played on Beebe Lake in 1929, as Balch Hall looms behind. The rink was approximately 200 by 80 feet, with 18-inch-high wooden boards. Engineering professor Johnny Parson raised $150 to help "build" the rink. In the background, a warming house called Johnny Parson's Club—also known as "Japes"—was a place where, for 5¢, people could check their shoes and get a warm cup of coffee. (Cornell University Archives.)

Seen here is the makeshift predecessor to the Zamboni. The ice was flooded by pumping in water from elsewhere on the lake. The horse-drawn scraper then helped shave down the ice, often followed by players smoothing the surface by hand. (Cornell University Archives.)

A *c.* 1929 game takes place on Beebe Lake. After a 1-0 loss to St. Lawrence, the *Ithaca Journal* noted, "Poor ice made good hockey impossible. . . . The ice was nursed along into something like fair condition. A wide crack ran across the rink, with the puck getting lost in it every few minutes. A large 'puddle' of water bordered the north side of the rink, and there were two or three holes along the boards." (Cornell University Archives.)

Nicky Bawlf coached Cornell from 1920 to 1947. Bawlf, who played professional hockey from 1910 to 1915 for Haileybury and Toronto of the NHA (predecessor to the NHL), also coached Canada's 1932 Olympic track and field team. "We liked Nicky, he was a good guy," said Dave Cutting, who played in the 1940s. "He had a bit of a swagger, he was kind of cocky. He seemed to be an ass chewer, but down in his heart, he would do anything for you."

15

Coach Nicky Bawlf (left) appears with goalie Ward Wannop and manager William McLean in 1939. After the 1939–40 season, Bawlf would give up his lacrosse-coaching duties to concentrate on running the intramural program. He continued to coach soccer and hockey. (Cornell University Archives.)

In this photograph of an early game, note the makeshift wooden boards surrounding the ice surface. Sometimes the ice was so soft, passes would get bogged down in water. Because of poor ice conditions, Cornell could not get any games in during all of the 1931–32 and 1932–33 seasons. "We changed our skates in that little lodge there," said Dave Cutting, class of 1948. "And you can imagine guys from Harvard skating in there [and] from these fancy schools. It was so primitive." (Cornell University Archives.)

Seen in this 1939 team photograph are, from left to right, the following: (kneeling) Robert Wiggans, Stanley Roberts, Glen Allen, Otto Poirier, unidentified, Kenneth Reed, and James Bostwick; (standing) Nicholas Bawlf (coach), Albert Bosson (co-captain), Carl Geiger, Augustus Nicholls, Clark Kimball, Raymond McElwee, Robert Killian, ? Bronkie, ? Ecker, and William McLean (manager). (Cornell University Archives.)

A 1947 team photograph. The equipment was a little better, but the Big Red remained stuck on Beebe Lake and, therefore, at a disadvantage. From left to right are the following: (first row) Irving Holcomb, Walter Schmidt, John Brady, Dave Cutting, and Joseph Louis; (second row) coach Arthur Boehringer, Robert Ellis, David McNair, Newton Burnett, and assistant manager Robert Corrigan. (*Cornellian*.)

The team practices on the Beebe Lake c. 1947. According to a *Cornell Daily Sun* article, the cracking in the ice surface got worse after World War II, when water was drawn from the lake to generate hydroelectric power. (*Cornellian.*)

Cornell gets in a practice any time it can, even in the dark of night. "We were like peasants," said Ray McElwee, captain in 1939–40. The 1947–48 team even tried alternate sites, playing at times on a rink at Dwyer's Dam, behind what became Oxley Equestrian Center. Athletic director Robert Kane attempted flooding the Lower Alumni Field, to disastrous results. The team went 0-4 in its last season before suspending the program until proper facilities could be built. (*Cornellian.*)

Two

PAUL PATTEN

THE REBIRTH OF A PROGRAM

While Ivy rival Dartmouth boasted of the Riley brothers and Dick Rondeau, and Harvard excited crowds with the Cleary brothers, Cornell's program was in mothballs.

Unable to sustain a team that relied on an all-too-often-unfrozen lake as its playing surface, Cornell shut down its hockey program pending the construction of an indoor facility with artificial ice. But without funding, there would be no construction. Four years passed, then five, then six, with no progress, and no hockey.

Then, at a Thanksgiving Day luncheon before the 1954 Cornell-Penn football game, alumnus Walter Carpenter told director of athletics Bob Kane that he might be interested in helping Cornell build a hockey rink. Carpenter was chairman of the DuPont Company and a 1910 graduate of Cornell. Several weeks of negotiations resulted in disappointment, however—in the end it was decided that Carpenter's money would fund the costs of a new engineering library instead. But Carpenter was concerned about disappointing his old friend Kane, and shortly thereafter he arranged for the Carpenter Foundation to underwrite the costs of a new rink as well. The $500,000 donation was originally announced as an anonymous gift.

The new pride of East Hill opened on March 21, 1957, with a match between the National Hockey League's (NHL) New York Rangers and the American Hockey League's (AHL) Rochester Americans, before 4,200 spectators. But the new rink did not necessarily lead to instant, rabid enthusiasm for the new Cornell program.

Picked to lead the reborn program was Paul Patten, who came from St. Lawrence and set about building the pieces one by one. The early years were filled with lopsided losses, and the team's first Ivy League win did not come until 1960–61, after 26 straight defeats. Cornell first played in its new building on December 14, 1957, a game against Lehigh, an even more loose band of hockey stragglers than the Big Red. Half of Lehigh's team failed to arrive for the first period, the game started 55 minutes late, and Lehigh fell behind 9-0. For the second period, Lehigh pressed into service some players from a Schenectady club team that had played the Cornell freshmen earlier in the day. The rest of the Lehigh team arrived in time for the third period. The Big Red got five goals from John Gillies and won 16-3, in front of 1,500 fans.

The second game of the season was also at home, a 7-1 loss to Norwich, played in front of what the *Ithaca Journal* deemed a "sparse crowd." By game three, a 13-1 drubbing at the hands of Princeton, the Big Red earned a scant half-sentence mention in the next day's papers. There would be just two more wins, another against Lehigh and one against Colgate, that first season.

The next two seasons were hardly better, but Cornell's fortunes began to change in the fall of 1960. The Big Red opened the season with a 9-0 victory over Penn in Philadelphia. It was the first shutout in the new program's history. The sophomore goalie who backstopped the victory, Laing Kennedy, went on to post nine more shutouts in his three seasons, but more important, he was the team's first legitimate star. His dazzling heroics in goal helped Cornell to its first winning record (13-5) in 1961–62, a season that finally marked Cornell's emergence from infancy.

This evolution was on full display in what would become the watershed moment in Cornell hockey history. The Big Red was playing well, with a 7-4 record in January 1962, and was headed toward perhaps the first winning record in the new program's history. People were beginning to take notice. Lynah Rink was regularly drawing crowds of 2,000–3,000 spectators.

As a meeting with Harvard—the long-dominant Ivy League team—approached, a palpable buzz began. Cornell had only beaten Harvard twice before in its history, but it was ancient history, with the last win coming in 1912. Earlier in the season, the Big Red lost at Harvard 5-1. But the Cornell squad was coming together, and an Ivy League crown was an actual possibility . . . if only the could beat Harvard.

And then, it happened. Well before game time, fans started lining up outside Lynah, eager to find a good seat inside. By the opening face-off, Lynah's innards were swelled with 4,200 spectators (4,500 according to some accounts), squeezed together in every way imaginable. Cornell won 2-1, and it was like a coronation as fans burst onto the ice to celebrate after the game.

"I'm by our own blue line with my stick all the way up in the air, jumping up and down," said Laing Kennedy. "And then the final buzzer goes off, and all I can remember is being flat on the ice."

Nothing was the same ever again.

The groundbreaking for a new $500,000 indoor ice rink occurred on June 5, 1956. Walter Carpenter's original donation came with one condition: he did not want his name on the building. Cornell's athletic director, Bob Kane, instead chose his former boss and Carpenter's former DuPont co-worker, James Lynah, to be the building's namesake. (*We're No. 1.*)

The new facility was designed by Van Storch, Evans, and Burkavage of Waverly, Pennsylvania, and constructed by Streeter Associates of Elmira. Lynah Rink was completed early in 1957. (Cornell University Archives.)

Lynah Rink was dedicated on April 6, 1957, and was officially named James D. Lynah Skating Hall, in honor of the 1905 Cornell graduate who was the university's director of athletics from 1935 to 1943. (Cornell University Archives.)

Paul Patten, former Notre Dame quarterback and coach of the hockey and football programs at St. Lawrence from 1946 to 1955, was picked to lead the reborn Cornell hockey program and supervise the construction of Lynah Rink. His early teams got pasted by seasoned Ivy League opponents, but it was a necessary learning experience. "We wanted to establish a strong program, so we had to be in a strong league," Patten told the *Cornell Daily Sun.*

The first team of the new era poses here. By and large, no players were recruited, and all were from New York and New England. From left to right are the following: (first row) John Detwiler, Pete Harrington, Joseph Kelsey, Bruce Wilton, Dave Foreman, and Howard Taylor; (second row) manager Brian Curtis, Hank Yates, John Coppage, Ed Vaughn, Lane Montesano, Vincent Gatto, Peter Blanchard, and coach Paul Patten; (third row) John Gillies, Roger Eastman, Edward Yates, Paul Marcus, John Volbrecht, and Mead Montgomery. (*Cornellian*.)

Early games at Lynah Rink were played before sparse crowds, as Cornell struggled to restart the program from scratch. The boards were bare, and there was no glass or netting along the sides to protect fans from the hazards of flying sticks and pucks. Today, fans watch from the same bench-style seating. (*Cornellian*.)

One of the early bright spots was John Gillies (9), who scored five goals against Lehigh in the team's inaugural game. Gillies then topped that performance with six goals in a rematch on March 8, 1958, setting a record that has stood the test of time. Success for Cornell hockey was elusive in the early years, though, as the program won just nine games in its first three seasons. (*Cornellian.*)

John Coppage (12) and Paul Marcus (8) scramble for the puck in a 1959 match at Lynah Rink. Early games included a 12-1 defeat by Yale, when Cornell allowed 72 shots on beleaguered goalies John Detwiler and Pete Wheelwright. In the first three seasons, the team posted a dismal 9-42-2 record. But coach Paul Patten's work did not go unnoticed. Jim Fullerton, Brown's coach, said, "I can't understand those Cornell guys. Every time we score they come back and play harder." (*Cornellian.*)

On February 3, 1962, Cornell, in the midst of its first winning season since World War II, entertained Harvard, a team that had not lost an Ivy League game in two years. Cornell had last beaten Harvard during the Taft administration. At least 4,200 fans packed Lynah Rink, the first "sellout" for a Cornell game. The Big Red's Jerry Kostandoff scored a power-play goal in the second period, and Cornell took a 2-0 lead on a goal by Webb Nichols at 8:02 of the third period. Harvard returned the tally three minutes later. Under a Crimson barrage, the Big Red held on for dear life, relying on star goalie Laing Kennedy, who made 48 saves. The final buzzer could not be heard over the din of the crowd. The *Ithaca Journal*'s Kenny Van Sickle noted, "The place had been bedlam after the first Cornell tally. It was worse after the second. And at the game's end the students really went berserk, invading the ice to shoulder off their heroes." Cornell hockey had arrived. And the Lynah mystique was officially born. (*Ithaca Journal*/Sol Goldberg.)

Cornell's fortunes had begun to turn with the class of 1963, which featured a goalie from Woodstock, Ontario, named Laing Kennedy. Known for his acrobatic saves, Kennedy, who started every game in his three seasons, would often stop 40 or more shots a game to preserve victories. He won three straight team Most Valuable Player (MVP) awards for his efforts. Kennedy went on to serve as Cornell athletic director from 1983 to 1994, and served as chair of the NCAA men's ice hockey committee. (*Cornellian.*)

The trainer of the era was the popular Joe DiLibero. "He always had a cigar stump hanging out of his mouth," said Laing Kennedy. DiLibero also worked as a bartender at a local establishment, and in an era without assistant coaches, acted as a go-between among players and Coach Patten. After DiLibero died suddenly on February 26, 1966, his friends established an award in his memory, which is given each season for "skilled efficiency, unselfish dedication, and hard-nosed competitive application." (Cornell University Archives.)

Jim Stevens, shown here battling for the puck, and other members of the class of 1964, including Jerry Kostandoff, Steve Poole, and George Walker, helped Patten's club continue to improve. Stevens once scored goals in nine straight games, a record that stood for almost 28 years. (*Cornellian*.)

Tragedy struck late in 1962 when John Velie, a member of the 1961–62 freshman team, died in an automobile accident in his hometown of Minneapolis during the holiday recess. His family created a memorial award to be presented to an outstanding member of the freshman squad.

Rudy Mateka (left) blocks a shot while Laing Kennedy tends goal. The 12-member class of 1963 helped Cornell make major strides toward respectability, beginning with their play as sophomores in the fall of 1960. "We were a very good freshman team," said Kennedy. "We just beat everybody, including our own varsity team. And I would say we were a very cocky group, hockey players that strutted around campus believing we were the saviors of Cornell hockey." Saviors or not, they were instrumental in Cornell's first-ever Ivy League victory, a 6-2 decision over Brown on February 11, 1961. The Big Red had dropped its first 26 straight Ivy contests. When the class of 1963 left Cornell, Paul Patten left too. He retired to run a golf course in Stroudsburg, Pennsylvania. Director of athletics Bob Kane said to Patten at his retirement banquet, "You have established a new dimension in excitement here during these revival years of hockey." (*Cornellian*.)

Three

NED HARKNESS
A College Hockey Dynasty

In six years as coach, Paul Patten made progress with the renewed Cornell program. But after the 1962–63 season had ended, Patten announced he was leaving to operate a golf course in Pennsylvania. He had planted the seeds, but said simply, "It's time."

It did not take long for Cornell to find the coach that was needed to take the team to the proverbial next level. Looking for a better situation for his family, Ned Harkness was ready to leave RPI, a place where he won a national championship in 1954. Named the Big Red's new coach on March 13, 1963, Harkness spent the next seven years turning Cornell hockey into the singular dominant force in the East.

The first season was modest—and, in fact, delayed. The Harkness era was set back a few days when the season opener against McGill, scheduled for November 23, was cancelled due to the assassination of President Kennedy. When the season finally got under way, the Big Red was mediocre and finished 12-10-1. The season ended at a sold-out Lynah Rink with a 3-2 overtime loss to Dartmouth, which gave the Indians (as they were then known) their 11th Ivy title in 28 years.

Of course, Rome was not built in a day, and neither is a hockey dynasty. But by the end of the Harkness era, the Big Red had compiled a ridiculous 163-27-2 record, including four straight ECAC tournament championships and two national championships, culminating in what has stood as the only perfect season of the modern era.

Harkness believed his style was simple: skate and forecheck like mad, and never stop moving. "Add some desire and the willingness to work together. That's it in a nutshell," he said. "You need those kids who aren't afraid to dig into the corners, too. If a player won't go into the corners he might as well take up checkers." Such is a common approach now, but not then.

Harkness also ruffled plenty of feathers. He never drank or smoked, but he was gruff and feisty with no use for small talk. He took grief around Eastern hockey for using an all-Canadian team. Harkness said he just wanted the best players. But no one could question his recruiting ability. He had a way of making people believe in him.

Back then, the East-West parochialism in college hockey was at its most pronounced. Few teams from the East ever saw teams from the West, and vice versa. There was no satellite television, no videotape. When East and West did meet in competition, in the NCAA tournament, the West largely dominated, leading Western teams to assume an attitude of superiority and condescension that Eastern squads resented, but which they all too often had to begrudgingly admit was warranted.

For all the rivalries with his Eastern counterparts, Harkness had to be praised for helping diminish that aura. From 1948, when the NCAA tournament began, until 1970, only four Eastern teams won the championship. Three of those teams were coached by Harkness. After Cornell won its 1967 semifinal against North Dakota 1-0, the opposing coach, Bill Selman, said, "They're very, very tough. They're rugged. They would have no trouble in our league. They were everything I heard they were, and so was Dryden." Selman was referring to young goaltender Ken Dryden, who by then was solidifying his reputation as an emerging superstar.

But it still was not always easy to earn respect. In 1969, even Harkness's old friend, Denver's Murray Armstrong, could not help himself from doubting the Cornell team. After his team had won its NCAA semifinal, and before Cornell was set to play Michigan Tech in theirs, Armstrong said, "Now we can start thinking about Tech." But Cornell won and met Denver in the finals.

The odds were stacked against Cornell that game, though. Playing in "shadowy, antiquated Broadmoor Arena," the Big Red, on one less day's rest, battling the high altitude, and playing without injured John Hughes and ineligible Dick Bertrand (too old according to NCAA rules), took a tie into the third period. Denver eventually pulled out a victory to take its second straight title. It was Harkness's most disappointing defeat.

Using that loss as motivation, and despite the departure of four all-Americans, Harkness pushed and prodded his 1969–70 team to a perfect 27-0 record heading into the NCAA tournament in Lake Placid. It was there that Harkness's trademark conditioning regimen was most evident. Trailing 1-0 entering the third period of the semifinal, Cornell held Wisconsin shotless in the final frame and won 2-1. Cornell thus set up a rematch with Clarkson, the team it had just defeated in the ECAC final, for the national championship. Sixty minutes and three Dan Lodboa goals later, Cornell's second national title and a perfect season were secured.

Within days, Harkness was gone, but he left a legacy since unmatched in college hockey.

To Ned Harkness, everything was important. To be big, you acted big. When he got to Ithaca, one of the first things he did was revamp Lynah Rink, enclosing the arena with glass above the boards, renovating the locker rooms, and hanging the banners of opposing teams. Harkness was also the first to encourage the school to print game programs and to get the pep band to play at hockey games. (Cornell University Archives.)

Between Kennedy and Dryden, there was goaltender Errol McKibbon, who manned the Big Red nets from 1963 to 1966. Here, in the first ECAC home game of the Harkness era, on December 10, 1963, sophomore McKibbon took it on the chin in a 7-0 loss to Clarkson. Steve Poole (7) takes the face-off, with George Walker (18) and Charlie Luther (14) standing guard. Walker was a First Team All-Ivy selection. (Cornell University Archives/Sol Goldberg.)

Harkness began recruiting right away, bringing in a class of 1967 stacked with players who would be integral to Cornell's rise to power. Among them were future all-American Harry Orr (left), Bob, Doug, and Dave Ferguson, Mike Doran, Murray Deathe, and Bob Kinasewich. In 1964–65, a Cornell squad that had no seniors but 13 sophomores earned its first ECAC playoff berth, closing the season with six straight wins before losing its postseason game in overtime to Brown.

The undefeated 1965–66 Cornell freshman team was loaded with four eventual all-Americans, including a future NHL Hall of Famer. Over its next three years, this group won three ECAC tournaments and lost just one home game. Among those who eventually saw significant time on varsity were, from left to right, the following: (first row, starting second from left) Pete Tufford, Bruce Pattison, Brian Cornell, and Ken Dryden; (second row) coach Jim Stevens, Bob McGuinn (9), and Ted Coviello (17). (Cornell Athletic Communications.)

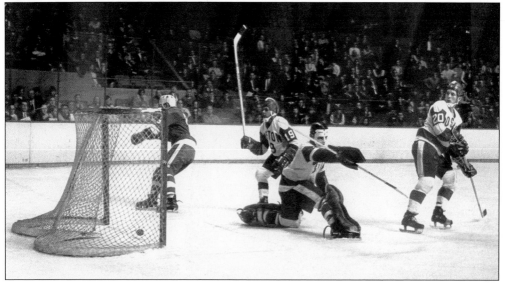

What became one of college hockey's fiercest rivalries began December 30, 1966, when Cornell and Boston University played to a 3-3 double-overtime tie at the Boston Arena Christmas Tournament. Cornell dominated the rivalry's early years. Here, Brian Cornell scores on Boston University's Wayne Ryan. (Cornell University Archives/Paul Weissman.)

Mike Doran (8) was a junior when he captained the 1965–66 team, which compiled a 22-5 season record to continue the meteoric rise of the program under Harkness. Cornell swept Brown, a nemesis in prior years, in a home-and-home series on the way to Cornell's first Ivy title. After losing the ECAC tournament final to Clarkson, the Big Red would have qualified for the NCAA tournament, but did not get a bid because of a dispute about academic standards between the NCAA and the Ivy League. (Sol Goldberg.)

Senior goaltender Dave Quarrie was set to start the 1966–67 season, but he hurt his ankle just before it began. So Harkness turned to sophomore goalie Ken Dryden (above), who proceeded to go 26-0-1 with a 1.46 goals-against average in leading Cornell to its first national championship. Quarrie took the team's only loss that season, 4-3 to Yale in overtime despite a large shot advantage for the Big Red. It was Cornell's last home loss for another 63 games. (*We're No. 1.*)

Ned Harkness (right) talks with John "Snooks" Kelley, who coached Boston College from 1946 to 1972. Cornell clobbered the Eagles 12-2 in the 1967 ECAC semifinals, setting a record for goals in an ECAC tournament game. Doug Ferguson scored four goals while playing with a broken thumb and took a six-stitch gash over his right eye during the game. Said Kelley, "When they're hot, they can make you look bad. They have the finest passing team in college hockey." (*We're No. 1.*)

Boston University's Serge Boily, a member of BU's famed Pinball Line, shoots as Cornell goalie Ken Dryden scrambles to get back in position. Cornell defeated BU 4-3 to win its first ECAC tournament championship. After the game, a Terrier fan lamented of Dryden, "He's just a sophomore." (*Cornell Daily Sun.*)

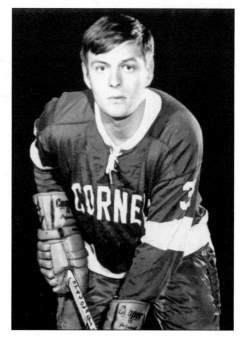

A student in the class of 1968, Walt "Skip" Stanowski compiled 72 points as a defenseman and was an all-American in his senior season. He was the only member of his class to play regularly for three seasons. Stanowski scored the only goal in Cornell's 1-0 win over North Dakota in the 1967 NCAA semifinals.

Ned Harkness's first big coup as head coach was the recruitment of the Ferguson brothers, twins Dave (left) and Doug (center), and Bob, out of Birsay, Saskatchewan. Here, the brothers celebrate with their father after winning the 1967 national championship. According to legend, Denver coach Murray Armstrong, a friend of Harkness, led the Fergusons to Cornell. Denver had no room for them, and Armstrong wanted to keep the brothers out of the hands of rival North Dakota. Harkness was aggressive in going into Canada to recruit the best players he could, more so than most of his contemporaries. Doug Ferguson scored a Cornell single-season record 37 goals in 1965–66 and became the Big Red's first all-American. In 1967, he was named Cornell's first ECAC Player of the Year. Doug finished with 91 goals and 187 points, Dave with 51 goals and 122 points, and Bob with 49 points. (*Ithaca Journal.*)

Coach Ned Harkness is lifted off the ice after the 1967 NCAA tournament championship in Syracuse. Following the game, an emotional Harkness thought back to his father, "Pop" Harkness, who had coached the Cornell freshman team until he died in 1964. Pop once prophetically told his son that the undefeated 1963–64 freshman team members were "going to be national champs." Said Ned, "Pop would have been proud of these boys." (Cornell Athletic Communications.)

The 1967 NCAA All-Tournament Team included, from left to right, Jim Quinn, Boston University; Tom Mikkola, Michigan State; and Cornell's Mike Doran, Harry Orr, Skip Stanowski, and Ken Dryden. (Cornell Athletic Communications.)

Brian Cornell fakes out sprawling Harvard defenseman Ben Smith—the future coach of Northeastern and the U.S. Women's Olympic team—then dekes goalie Bill Diercks as he scores in a 7-2 win at Lynah Rink in 1967–68. Cornell had a 23-game winning streak, capped by a 6-3 win over Boston College in the ECAC tournament championship game. The Big Red lost its NCAA semifinal to North Dakota 3-1 and finished the season 27-2. (Sol Goldberg.)

While at RPI, Ned Harkness not only won the 1954 NCAA hockey tournament but also earned a de facto national championship in lacrosse. Eventually, Harkness took on lacrosse duties at Cornell, too, coaching the team for three seasons and going 35-1. After winning a 1967 hockey playoff game against Brown, Harkness did not stay to celebrate; he headed to a 10:30 p.m. lacrosse practice. In 1969, he handed the lacrosse reins to Richie Moran, who stayed at Cornell for 30 years. (*We're No. 1.*)

Something important was almost always on the line when Cornell and Boston University met in fierce, tense battles. Though the Big Red controlled the rivalry, never losing into the 1970s, goalie Ken Dryden (above) reserved a reverence for the match-ups against the Terriers. In his book *The Game*, Dryden said: "They were the necessary other side in many of my most fundamental moments, the inspiration and competitive prod for them, irrevocably and fondly associated with them. . . . In the first period of the [1967] ECAC final, I survived great pressure to learn something about myself I needed to know; then, during the warm-up for the NCAA championship game, feeling skates, pads, gloves, and stick move the way they never did, I could feel myself a real goalie for the first time. . . . When a career ends, when the passion of the game subsides, towards a good opponent you only feel gratitude." (Cornell University Archives.)

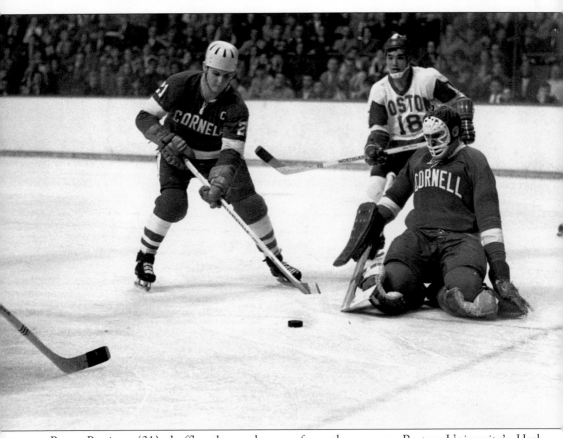

Bruce Pattison (21) shuffles the puck away from the cage as Boston University's Herb Wakabayashi looks for a chance in the ECAC semifinals at Boston Garden on March 7, 1969. Wakabayashi assisted on two third-period goals as BU rallied to tie the game. Cornell then defeated the Terriers 3-2 on Kevin Pettit's goal 31 seconds into overtime. (Cornell University Archives.)

Dan Lodboa (14) became an all-American after Coach Harkness converted him to defense at the start of the 1968–69 season. Lodboa later won the 1970 NCAA Most Outstanding Player Award. (Cornell University Archives.)

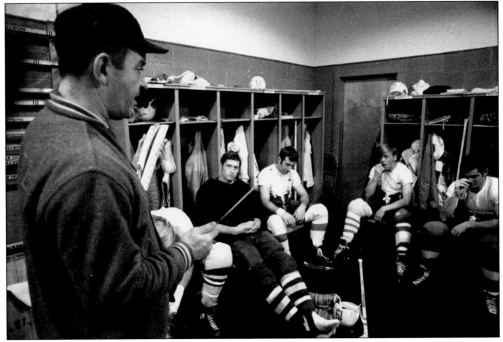

In the Lynah locker room, Harkness addresses, from left to right, Dick Bertrand, Dan Lodboa, John Hughes, and Brian McCutcheon. Bertrand and McCutcheon must have listened well, as they went on to become head coaches at Cornell. (Cornell University Archives.)

Brian Cornell co-captained the 1968–69 team. After losing its first road game, the Big Red ripped off 25 straight victories, culminating in a 4-2 win over Harvard in the ECAC championship game. A highlight of the season came just after Christmas, at the Syracuse Invitational. There, Cornell defeated Minnesota-Duluth—with Glenn "Chico" Resch in goal—2-1, and overcame a 3-0 third-period deficit to defeat St. Lawrence in the championship game. (Cornell University Archives.)

During the March 14, 1969 NCAA tournament semifinal versus Michigan Tech, Cornell defenseman Gordie Lowe scored twice, including the winner at 1:40 of overtime. "I practiced that play every day all year. I feel beautiful," he said afterward. Michigan Tech's Al Karlander scored all three of his team's goals, the first one an NCAA-record seven seconds into the game. It was the only time Ken Dryden ever allowed a hat trick in his college or NHL career. (*Cornell Daily Sun.*)

Harkness considered pulling Dryden from the 1969 NCAA championship game against Denver, because his netminder was clearly fatigued from lack of sleep after having played an overtime game the day before. But how could Harkness do that to a senior? After the game, Dryden went to a party for Denver's team at their invitation, where he congratulated his opponents and was given a standing ovation by those in attendance. Perhaps they were just glad Cornell's goaltender was finally graduating. (Cornell Athletic Communications.)

43

Pete Tufford was one of the four all-Americans, along with Ken Dryden, Bruce Pattison, and Brian Cornell, who graduated following the Big Red's loss in the 1969 NCAA tournament championship game. Tufford, a talented forward, compiled 160 points in three seasons, and later was a longtime commentator on Cornell radio broadcasts. Following the 27-2 season in 1968–69, prognosticators figured Cornell would still be in the mix in 1969–70 but would not be as strong because of the loss of talent.

Ned Harkness (second from right) glumly accepts the 1969 NCAA runner-up trophy from an NCAA official (far left) at the historic Broadmoor Arena in Colorado Springs, Colorado. Coach Harkness is flanked by players Bruce Pattison (second from left) and Brian Cornell. The Big Red lost the title game to Denver 4-3, as the Pioneers, playing on an extra-day's rest, won their second straight championship. "We know Ned wanted to win this one badly, and we're disappointed that we couldn't do it for him," said outgoing all-American Pete Tufford. (*Cornell Daily Sun.*)

A thoughtful, introspective athlete, Ken Dryden took time away from hockey to complete law school, and later went on to a career as a lawyer, executive, and politician. He also happened to win six Stanley Cups with the Montreal Canadiens and five Vezina Trophies as the NHL's top goaltender. His greatest memories came at Boston Garden, where he was 10-0 while at Cornell and where he had many unforgettable NHL playoff series against the Boston Bruins. "Old and dirty, not unlike sports neighbor Fenway Park, but its quirks unsoftened, uneulogized by the romance of baseball, and what makes Fenway a cherished anomaly makes the Garden an embarrassment. For me it is special. It has to do with three ECAC championships and 2,000 Cornell fans sounding as people on a pilgrimage sound. . . . Boston Garden is like a disheveled friend," Dryden remarked in his book *The Game*.

Cornell captain John Hughes splits St. Lawrence defenders during a 7-2 win in the ECAC Holiday Festival championship game at Madison Square Garden on December 23, 1969. St. Lawrence had upset previously unbeaten Boston College in the semifinals, while Cornell had topped Rensselaer Polytechnic 9-0. Cornell also crushed St. Lawrence two other times that season, including an ECAC quarterfinal playoff win at Lynah. (*Cornell Daily Sun.*)

After Ken Dryden and three fellow all-Americans graduated from Cornell in 1969, most figured the Big Red hockey dominance would be over. But stepping in between the pipes to replace the six-foot-four Dryden, also known as "The Big Kid," was a perfect contrast, the five-foot-five Brian Cropper (left), also known as "The Little Kid." Cropper, donning a lacrosse mask, started every one of his team's games during his junior year, as Cornell went a perfect 29-0. (*Cornell Daily Sun.*)

In a February game at Dartmouth, Cornell's perfect season of 1969–70 was nearly ruined, until the team rallied with two late third-period goals to win 3-2. On March 4, 1970, 11 days later, Cornell held nothing back in the rematch and rolled up a 14-0 win. Dan Lodboa (14) did not score here, but the man in front looking for the rebound, Bob Aitchison (8), already had four goals in the game. Aitchison, mostly a third-line checking forward, turned in the offensive highlight of his career. The Dartmouth goalie is Dale Dunning. (Cornell University Archives.)

Mark Davis (center) handles the puck while teammates Ron Simpson (far left) and Brian McCutcheon contend with St. Lawrence at Lynah Rink. The 1969–70 season was another perfect one at home. From 1967 to 1972, the Big Red won 63 straight home games. "Teams were scared coming in there," said coach Ned Harkness. "They were intimidated before they came through the doors." (Cornell University Archives.)

Cornell defeated Harvard 6-5 in the 1970 ECAC tournament semifinals. It was another close game with a clutch conclusion for a team that, although not as talented as some of its predecessors, was headed for a perfect season. (Cornell University Archives.)

Harvard's Ralph "Cooney" Weiland (right) congratulates Ned Harkness after Cornell defeated the Crimson 6-5 in the 1970 ECAC tournament semifinals. Harkness fostered an "us versus them" mentality when it came to the Boston schools, but in truth he had respect for those programs, and they in turn respected Cornell. (Cornell University Archives.)

The "Buzz-Saw Line" of sophomores Ed Ambis (17), Craig Brush (11), and Doug Stewart sparked a comeback in the 1970 ECAC championship game against Clarkson. (Cornell University Archives.)

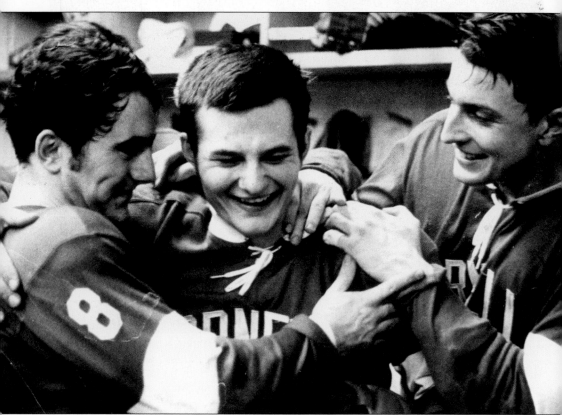

Ed Ambis (center) is mobbed by teammates Bob Aitchison (left) and Bill Duthie after Cornell won the 1970 ECAC championship title over Clarkson. Ambis's little-used, all-sophomore fourth line was put in for a spark in the second period and ultimately created Ambis's game-tying goal. In the third, John Hughes thought he had scored the game-winner, but referee Giles Threadgold ruled he was "a quarter-inch" offside. Not to be denied, Hughes scored again, for keeps, off a scramble in front with 14 seconds left. Cornell's fourth straight ECAC title kept the perfect season intact as the team headed to Lake Placid for the NCAA tournament. The games in Lake Placid were to be played in the quaint Olympic Arena, which barely fit 2,000 people, a fact that led to grumbling from many fans who were annoyed the NCAA would approve a location merely to serve Lake Placid's public-relations efforts as that city tried to win its bid to host the 1976 Winter Olympics. (*Ithaca Journal.*)

Steve Giuliani, one of a number of players Ned Harkness successfully moved to forward from defense, skates against Wisconsin in the 1970 semifinals. (*Cornell Daily Sun.*)

Brian McCutcheon (9) shoots on Wisconsin's Wayne Thomas in the 1970 NCAA semifinals. Using its trademark swarming forechecking, Cornell put up double-digit shot totals, while holding the Badgers shotless in the third period, and rallied for a 2-1 win. "Their checking was too much," said Badger coach Bob Johnson (not yet the legend he would become). "They just skate too well." (*Cornell Daily Sun.*)

51

Dave Westner scores on Bruce Bullock at 13:37 of the second period of the 1970 NCAA championship game at Lake Placid. Westner's goal tied the score at 3-3 and set the stage for Dan Lodboa's third-period heroics. Because of the venue's limited seating capacity, most interested fans listened to the game on radio back in Ithaca, after a Syracuse public-television station's efforts to broadcast the final were thwarted when the NCAA asked for too much money in rights fees. (*Cornell Daily Sun.*)

Cornell defenseman Dan Lodboa finishes off a third-period hat trick with a dramatic two-man-down shorthanded goal against Clarkson in the 1970 NCAA championship game. The final score was 6-4, and Cornell capped a perfect season. (*Cornell Daily Sun.*)

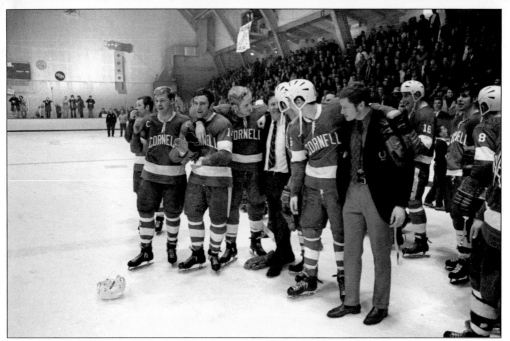

Coach Ned Harkness (center) and the senior players share a moment as Cornell awaits the presentation of its 1970 championship trophy. (Cornell University Archives.)

Accepting the 1970 national championship trophy from an NCAA official (far right) are (clockwise from left) Cornell players Dan Lodboa and John Hughes, head coach Ned Harkness, and coach Dick Bertrand. Also standing with the group are Harkness's daughter Alice and an unidentified young Cornell fan (front). (Cornell University Archives.)

Steve Giuliani celebrates the championship in style. The rowdy Ithacans who had earlier squeezed into the tiny arena to watch the culmination of a perfect season "poured out into the streets of Lake Placid, to start celebrations which continued into the early morning hours," wrote the *Ithaca Journal*'s Jerry Langdon. And in an unintentionally ironic comment (in retrospect), Langdon added, "Lake Placid might never see such a happy bunch of conventioneers again." (*We're No. 1.*)

The team returned home on a snowy day to a large throng of Faithful. Here, Ned Harkness and his daughter Alice enjoy the great reception. Meanwhile, rumors swirled over Harkness's future. Some media sources already had the coach signing a contract with the NHL's Detroit Red Wings, something he denied on the eve of the national championship game. But Harkness—fresh off a perfect season, his third NCAA championship, and with nothing left to prove in college hockey— did indeed sign a contract with the Red Wings soon after returning to Ithaca. (Cornell University Archives.)

Four

DICK BERTRAND

THE HIGH-FLYING YEARS

Dick Bertrand was a police officer in Canada taking night courses at York University. After playing an exhibition game at Cornell in late 1965, Bertrand called coach Ned Harkness and asked if he could come to Cornell. Bertrand played three years for the Big Red and served as team captain, before, at the age of 29, he was persuaded by Harkness to take over following the perfect 29-0 season of 1969–70.

But replacing a legend is never easy. "There was no place to go but down," Bertrand said. Try as he might to keep the Cornell engine going, the odds were going to be stacked against him: players getting used to playing for a former teammate, the ever-increasing competition as Eastern hockey improved, and the pressure from a fan base and a school that came to expect winning all the time.

Even so, Bertrand's teams fared quite well, especially at first.

Playing with much of the nucleus from the 1970 national championship team, Cornell went 22-5 in 1970–71. After starting 0-2 in the ECAC, the Big Red won the next eight and eventually made it to the championships at Boston Garden, before a disappointing loss to Clarkson.

The following season also held much promise, as the top recruits, especially forwards, kept coming in. Cornell rode into Boston Garden in 1971–72 with an eight-game winning streak, and made it nine straight by easily disposing of New Hampshire. But in what would be the first sign of a true epochal shift in the East, Cornell lost its first significant game to Boston University . . . ever.

Since the two teams first met in the semifinals of the 1966 ECAC tournament, Cornell simply owned Boston University. Over the five seasons following 1966, a span that included ECAC finals and NCAA finals, the Big Red went 10-0-1 over the Terriers, including nine straight wins, before a loss in the ECAC tournament consolation game in 1971. Brushing it off as a game of little significance—and despite the fact that BU won the 1971 national championship—Cornell defeated the Terriers at the Syracuse Invitational in 1971–72, and again later that season in Boston. The "rivalry" stood at 12-1-1 in Cornell's favor.

But when Cornell and BU faced off in the 1972 ECAC championships, the final outcome would be quite different. Led by feisty forwards like John Danby, Ron Anderson, and Don Cahoon, the Terriers defeated Cornell 4-1 in the title game. The tide had turned.

Of course, it was not quite over for the Big Red, as the team made the NCAA tournament, also played that year at Boston Garden. In the semifinals, Cornell was an underdog, and goalie Dave Elenbaas had pulled his hamstring in the BU loss in the ECAC tournament. But after being treated with painkillers, Elenbaas helped the Big Red steamroll over Denver 7-2 as Dave Westner scored four times against embattled Pioneers goalie Ron Grahame. Cornell was said to have a "huge" size disadvantage, with Denver averaging about 185 pounds a man, to Cornell's 175.

That only set up another chance for BU to show who was the new boss in the East. The Terriers won back-to-back titles by shutting out the Big Red 4-0 in the NCAA final—the first time Cornell had been shut out in 225 games.

In a six-year span, Cornell had made the NCAA finals four times, winning both times the team played the Thursday semifinal, and losing both times it played the Friday semifinal.

Still, the Big Red shook it off and racked up another big season (23-5-1) in 1972–73. Led by Elenbaas, Bill Murray, Carlo Ugolini, and George Kuzmicz, and with BU rebuilding following the retirement of coach Jack Kelley, Cornell steamrolled its way down the stretch, going unbeaten in 12 games to win its fifth ECAC tournament championship.

Again in Boston for the NCAA tournament, Cornell met up with an emerging Wisconsin team under the tutelage of Bob Johnson. And for all the monumental wins in Boston Garden, the Big Red faced its most crushing defeat. Down 5-2 in the third, the Badgers rallied, with Dean Talafous scoring the tying goal in the closing minute. After Cornell dominated overtime, Talafous scored again in the closing minute, capping the Big Red collapse. Wisconsin went on to win the West's first NCAA title since 1969 and became a dynasty of its own, while Cornell's dynasty was officially over, even if neither program really knew it at the time.

Despite some 20-win seasons and a whole lot of goals, it was seven years before Cornell's next ECAC final, ECAC championship, or NCAA tournament appearance.

Two years after that, in 1982, Dick Bertrand stepped down.

The year before, Dick Bertrand was the captain. Now he was the head coach of his former teammates. (*Cornell Daily Sun.*)

Brian McCutcheon scores while Carlo Ugolini celebrates in an exhibition game against the U.S. National Team on November 2, 1970. Defending for Team USA are goalie Mike Curran, Don Ross (5), and Herb Brooks (4), who would soon begin a coaching career that included three national championships and a 1980 Olympic gold medal. (*Cornell Daily Sun.*)

Goalie Brian Cropper and the rest of the championship-team holdovers lost their first two league games, but quickly turned it around in 1970–71, clobbering New Hampshire and Boston College to take the ECAC Holiday Festival in Boston. Cornell went 22-5 but ultimately fell short of the NCAAs for the first time in five years. (*Cornell Daily Sun.*)

Ray Ranta was a five-foot-eight forward who was MVP of the freshman team in 1969–70. Ineligible the first semester of his sophomore year, he debuted in a 2-1 loss at Clarkson. Ranta played well the rest of the season, but those 13 games were all he ever played. On February 27, 1971, in a game against Princeton at Lynah, Ranta scored four straight second-period goals, tying a record set by Pete Tufford in 1966 and not equaled since. (Larry Baum.)

Dick Bertrand (right) appears with Doc Kavanagh, a renowned athletic trainer who held patents on safer football headgear and hockey shoulder pads. Born in Ireland, where he served in the army during World War I, Kavanagh came to Cornell from St. Lawrence to become head trainer. Kavanagh arrived at Cornell in 1937, after working as a trainer for the 1936 U.S. Olympic team. He retired in 1966, but later came back to help the hockey program. He passed away in 1985. (Cornell Athletic Communications.)

In a highlight from Bertrand's first season, Kevin Pettit scores the game-tying goal with 15 seconds left in a match against Harvard. In overtime, Cornell would defeat the Crimson on a shorthanded goal. Harvard had won its first seven games of the 1970–71 season and had been considered the class of the East. Though the team cooled off considerably as the season wore on, the Crimson would go to the NCAA tournament in Cooney Weiland's final year as coach, while the Big Red would not. (Larry Baum.)

Bill Duthie scores Cornell's only goal in a 2-1 overtime loss at Clarkson in 1971. The game held significance not only in avenging Clarkson's loss in the previous year's national championship game, but also in marking the first regular-season meeting between the teams since the fall of 1966. Clarkson coach Len Ceglarski called it "the greatest college hockey game I've ever seen." The next season, Clarkson broke Cornell's 63-game Lynah Rink winning streak. The famed bell at Clarkson Arena (later known as Walker Arena) can be seen under the scoreboard and can still be heard ringing in the ears of many terrorized opponents. (Larry Baum.)

Larry Fullan sails through the air but just misses netting a goal. Cornell had plenty of goals in this game, however, defeating Providence 11-1 in the ECAC quarterfinal at Lynah Rink in March 1972. Fullan was the star of a dynasty that had gone into its waning years. From 1969 to 1972, he scored 57 goals and 165 points. Fullan's 63 points in 1972 led the Big Red for the second straight season, and he was named an all-American. (Cornell University Archives/Sol Goldberg.)

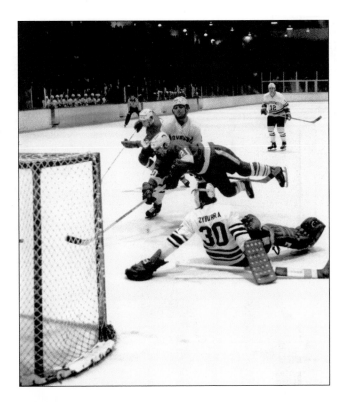

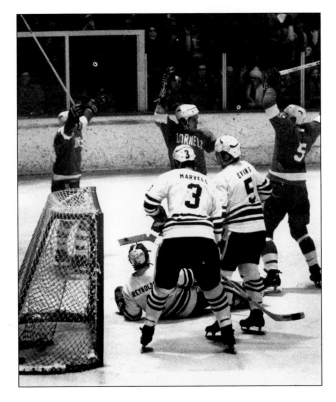

Bob Murray (center background) adds another goal to the tally in Cornell's win over Providence in the 1972 ECAC quarterfinal. Bill Murray (far right), who assisted on the goal, was a three-sport athlete at Cornell. He was a soccer tri-captain as a sophomore, and kicked three field goals in a football game, a school record that stood into the 21st century. In 1973, Bill was an All-Ivy and All-ECAC defenseman in hockey, and later he served as assistant hockey coach under Lou Reycroft. (Cornell University Archives/Sol Goldberg.)

Dave Elenbaas succeeded Brian Cropper in goal, turning in two standout seasons, as Cornell made the NCAAs in 1972 and 1973. One of the few blips in 1972–73 was a 9-0 loss to Boston University. The game was later forfeited to Cornell after the Big Red alerted the NCAA to the potential ineligibility of BU's Dick Decloe. For Cornell, it was justice after its freshman Peter Titanic was similarly declared ineligible. BU forfeited 11 games in all; years of bitterness ensued. (*Cornell Daily Sun.*)

Bob Murray (20) watches another goal for the Big Red, as the team defeats RPI 9-3 at Lynah in the 1973 ECAC quarterfinal playoffs. Cornell went on to defeat Boston College 3-2 to win the ECAC championship, its fifth. Cornell started wearing white jerseys at home during this season. (Russell Hamilton.)

Wisconsin's Stan Hinkley (center) celebrates the tying goal with five seconds left in regulation in the 1973 NCAA tournament semifinals. The goal scorer, Dean Talafous, jumps in the right background after converting a three-on-one break. Talafous later won the game by scoring again with 33 seconds remaining in overtime, after Cornell had dominated the extra session. It was a crushing loss for the Big Red, who led 5-2 on a Bill Murray goal 40 seconds into the third period. Of almost equal significance was the presence of Wisconsin's own brand of faithful fans, 2,000 singing, jolly Midwesterners who had traveled to Boston with a 70-piece band, complete with on-ice cheerleaders and something known as a "sieve" chant. When Cornell took a 5-2 lead early in the third, the *Cornell Daily Sun*'s Bill Howard wrote, "For a few blessed moments, the Badger Band in the first deck was silent." But not for long. (University of Wisconsin.)

Bill Murray (left) and Dave Groulx show off Cornell's new uniforms, unveiled in 1973–74. These uniforms were worn for three seasons before the Big Red returned to its classic style in 1976–77. In 1978–79, coach Dick Bertrand updated the look with the red sleeves at home and the black-outlined letters. Those jerseys remained, removing the bear logo from the shoulders by the mid-1980s, until 1987–88, when former captain Brian McCutcheon came back as head coach and reinstated the classic style. (Russell Hamilton.)

George Kuzmicz was an All-ECAC and all-American defenseman in 1973–74. He broke his jaw in a game at Harvard in January of his senior year, but returned to play wearing a modified football helmet. That season featured indications the dynasty was over, including the Big Red's first sub-20-win season in nine years. Also, Cornell went through embarrassing NCAA sanctions after it was discovered that a booster had paid for two recruits to fly to Boston to see Cornell in the ECACs. The Big Red was placed on probation for one season.

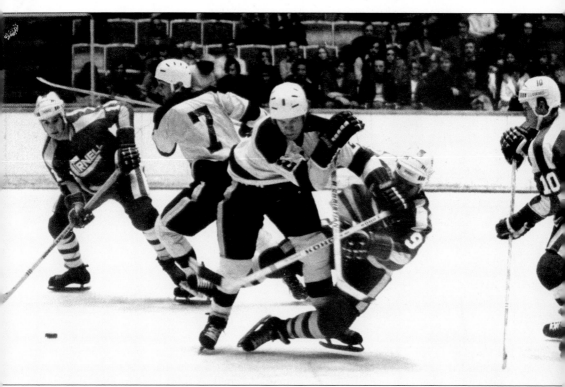

Cornell's John Harper (11), Dave Groulx (9), and Brian Campbell (10) skate against Colgate at the 1973 Syracuse Invitational. Among those defending for Colgate is Mike Milbury (7), who went on to a lengthy career in the NHL as a defenseman, coach, and general manager. The Big Red trio of Harper, Groulx and Campbell formed an all-sophomore line in 1973–74. All became 100-point scorers before they were through, and Campbell became a captain on the 1975–76 team. The 1973–74 team lost to Harvard 7-4 at Lynah Rink late in the season, as the Crimson snapped Cornell's streak of eight straight Ivy League titles. Cornell lost the ECAC semifinals to BU that season. (Cornell University Archives/Sol Goldberg.)

Jim Vaughan (1974–1977) left Cornell as one of the school's top career scorers (154 points). His 68 points led the team in 1975–76, and his five shorthanded goals that season set a school mark. Vaughan's brother Dan played just one game for Cornell. A third brother, Don, skated at St. Lawrence, and later served as assistant coach at Cornell from 1988 to 1990, before becoming head coach at Colgate. In 1975–76 Cornell lost the ECAC semifinals for a third straight season. (*Cornell Daily Sun.*)

Dave Ambrosia drives to the net during the 1976–77 season. Note the opposing team banners, which for a time lived on the west wall, and the Spirit of '76 American flag. (*Cornell Daily Sun.*)

Mark Trivett, who collected 52 goals and 95 points in his college career, captained the 1976–77 squad, along with Freddie Tomczyk and Jim Vaughan. That team, paced by 78 points from sophomore Lance Nethery, fostered a new era of explosive offense at Cornell. The Big Red posted double-digit goal totals in five games during 1976–77, including an 11-8 win against Clarkson at Lynah, but the team ultimately lost in the ECAC semifinals for a fourth straight season. (Larry Baum.)

Cornell's goaltending in the mid-1970s was not quite up to the standards of Big Red lore, partly due to the period's high-flying offensive nature, but that era did feature the first painted mask in Cornell history, worn here by Steve Napier. Also pictured is defenseman Bruce Marrett (2), a part of one of the three 3-brother combinations who have played for the Big Red. Bruce joined his brothers Doug and Brian at Cornell, forming another threesome to go along with the Fergusons and Fullans. (*Cornell Daily Sun.*)

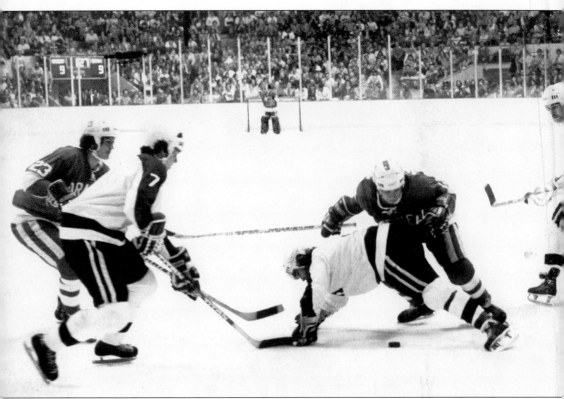

A Cornell player tries to sidestep the hip check of a New Hampshire defender during the 1977 ECAC semifinals at Boston Garden. The scoreboard in the background reads 9-9 (goals, not shots). In what would be Cornell's fourth straight ECAC semifinal loss, the Big Red and New Hampshire—the two most potent offenses of the era—rang up nine goals apiece, then went scoreless into a second overtime. "I just remember being so tired in the last OT period," said Cornell defenseman Peter Shier. The Wildcats' Ralph Cox had scored the game's tying goal, and Bob Gould netted the game-winner. "I was on for the goal and my legs just couldn't move anymore. Ralph and I played together in Europe a few years after that. He remembers the exact same feeling. The guys that played, played a lot. . . . So close yet so far." (*Cornell Daily Sun*.)

Peter Shier was an all-American in 1977–78, when he tied Dan Lodboa's season record for goals by a defenseman with 24, and set a career record with 48. "You'll never see the wide-open play of the '70s again," Shier said. "I liked to go with the puck. My teammates said I was one of the best forecheckers on the team. . . . Not many defensemen from that era made pro because we were all pretty lousy at defense." (Larry Baum.)

Lance Nethery passes to Roy Kerling in a December 1977 game against New Hampshire at Lynah Rink. This was a common sight, as Nethery racked up 60 assists and Kerling had 29 goals. Combined, the duo totaled 52 goals and 142 points in that season alone. (Cornell Athletic Communications.)

Lance Nethery (left), the 1977–78 ECAC Player of the Year, graduated in 1979 as the all-time leading scorer in both Cornell and ECAC history, with 271 points. Mark Weiss (far right) had 20 goals, before his tragic death in a car accident following the season. Roy Kerling (background) scored 200 points in his career. With the contributions of freshman Brock Tredway, the 1977–78 team had the most goals per game (7.2) in modern NCAA history. The Big Red went 262 games (1972–1982) without being shut out. (C. W. Pack.)

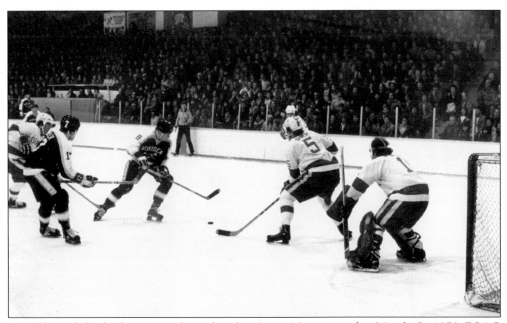

Pete Shier defends the net with goaltender Steve Napier in the March 7, 1978 ECAC quarterfinal game against Providence at Lynah Rink. The Friars won 8-5, marking the first home playoff loss in Cornell history. (*Cornell Daily Sun.*)

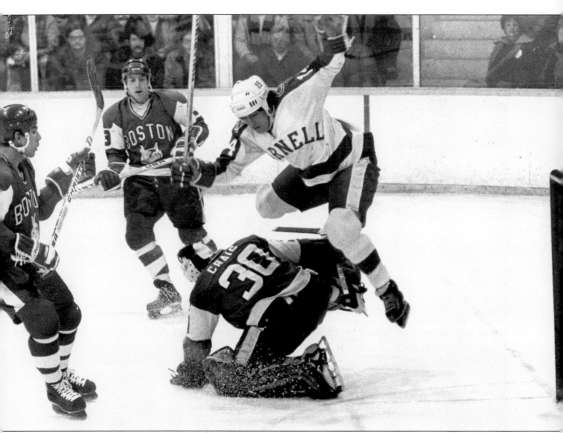

Peter Whiting is stopped by Boston University—and future U.S. Olympic team—goalie Jim Craig at Lynah Rink on January 6, 1979. Cornell won the game 5-1 to snap a nine-game losing streak to the Terriers, a team they had once dominated. After going 1-12-1 against Cornell between 1965 and 1972 (with the only win coming in a consolation game), the Terriers had since turned the tables on the rivalry. BU was rebuilding in 1978–79, however, after winning the 1978 national championship, and the Big Red went on to win the next six meetings, including this one. The last of those victories came at home in 1982–83; it would be the last meeting between the teams at Lynah Rink for almost 20 years. The next season, BU snapped Cornell's run with a win at Walter Brown Arena, and soon thereafter, the Terriers split from the ECAC to become part of the new Hockey East Association. (Cornell University Archives/Jon Crispin.)

Dave Ambrosia scored 129 points for the Big Red from 1975 to 1978 and was a captain during his senior year. (Larry Baum.)

Capping what is considered perhaps the most legendary game in the extraordinary history of Lynah Rink, Rob Gemmell (far left) scores in overtime to defeat Providence in the 1979 ECAC tournament quarterfinals. Cornell was down 5-1 midway through the third period when a historic comeback began. With his team still up 5-4 in the closing minute, Providence's Randy Wilson missed a wide-open net. The Big Red's Lance Nethery proceeded to score the game-tying goal with 13 seconds remaining. Cornell later lost in the semifinals. (Cornell Athletic Communications.)

Roy Kerling scores on Dartmouth goalie Bob Gaudet in 1980. Gaudet went on to a distinguished coaching career at Brown, making an NCAA tournament appearance, before returning to coach at his alma mater. (Cornell University Archives/Jon Crispin.)

After knocking off top seed Boston College, Cornell defeated No. 2 seed Providence in the 1980 ECAC semifinals. Note the helmet cages; this was the first year full shields or cages were encouraged by the NCAA. The next year, they were required equipment. (*Cornell Daily Sun.*)

Cornell went seven years without an ECAC title before its improbable run to the 1980 championship. Along the way, the Big Red, after barely qualifying for the playoffs, defeated the top three seeds in the field. It would be the last championship under Dick Bertrand. (Cornell Athletic Communications.)

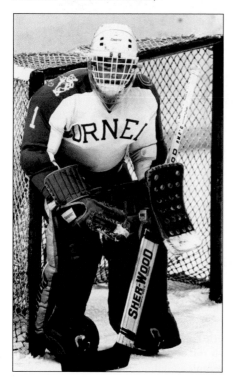

Darren Eliot had a phenomenal run during his freshman campaign in 1979–80. Eliot replaced sophomore Brian Hayward, who had gotten sick early in the season. Eliot, and the team at large, had an up-and-down year and needed wins in the last two games just to make the ECAC playoffs as a No. 8 seed. Cornell won the Boston University game 6-5 in overtime after blowing a 5-0 lead, and the team rode that momentum to an ECAC tournament championship. (Cornell Athletic Communications.)

Brian Hayward began anew the tradition of Cornell goaltending excellence when he came in as a freshman in 1978–79, a season highlighted by his win over BU, the team's first victory against the Terriers in seven years. Hayward's sophomore season was derailed by mononucleosis, and he split time with Darren Eliot during his junior season. But in 1981–82, Hayward carried the load as a senior and turned in an all-American season. He went on to play 357 games in the NHL. (Cornell Athletic Communications.)

Roy Kerling (20), John Olds (19), and Brock Tredway (7) battle a powerful Northern Michigan team in the 1980 NCAA semifinals in Providence. The opponents here are Walt Kyle (27), who was an assistant coach in the NHL before becoming head coach at NMU; Don Waddell (4), a future NHL executive; Tom Laidlaw (2), who played 705 NHL games; and goalie Steve Weeks, who played 296 NHL games. (*Cornell Daily Sun.*)

Roy Kerling (far left) and Jim Gibson (21) celebrate after scoring in the closing seconds of the 1980 NCAA semifinal game against Northern Michigan. The Big Red still lost 5-4, in its first NCAA tournament game in seven years. (Cornell Athletic Communications.)

Cornell trailed 3-0 before rallying to defeat Colgate 4-3 in the 1981 ECAC tournament semifinals at Boston Garden. Cornell players pictured include Paul Geiger (3), Tim Strawman (4), Geoff Dervin (15), and Jeff Baikie (23). At left is Colgate goalie Guy Lemonde. (*Cornell Daily Sun.*)

The Big Red finished first in the Ivy group during the 1980–81 regular season, and made it to the tournament championship game. Here, Jeff Baikie scores on Providence goalie Mario Proulx in the ECAC final, which many had predicted Cornell would win. But the Big Red lost 8-4. No one could have imagined it at the time, but this was Cornell's last trip to the Garden for another four years. (*Cornell Daily Sun.*)

Brock Tredway, cut from the team as a freshman in 1977–78, played with the junior varsity until the Big Red lost its first three ECAC games. Starting on the varsity squad's fourth line, Tredway gradually worked his way up the charts and had two four-goal games before season's end. Four years later, he left Cornell as the school's all-time leading goal scorer with 113, one per game. Tredway was named to the Cornell Athletic Hall of Fame in 1989. (Cornell Athletic Communications.)

Five

LOU REYCROFT
A TIME OF TRANSITION

When Dick Bertrand stepped down after the 1981–82 season, the Cornell program was trying to refind itself. The Big Red was coming off its first losing season in 21 years, with just one ECAC championship in the last nine. And it was facing a time when the balance of power in the East was slipping further and further away from the Ivy League schools.

The task of handling the situation was given to Bertrand's assistant, Lou Reycroft, a former goaltender at Brown. The task was not easy and was made harder by the changing forces happening right within the conference.

Before the 1983–84 season, six teams announced their intention to leave the ECAC and form a new conference, Hockey East. Boston University, Boston College, Providence, New Hampshire, Northeastern, and Maine formed Hockey East as a preemptive move made in response to a push by Ivy League teams to break off from the ECAC. The Ivy League schools had been planning to form another league that would include a subset of schools willing to adhere to Ivy League academic standards. Instead, the Hockey East schools split off from the conference following the 1983–84 season. The break-up of the ECAC was far from amicable, and the rift caused an ugliness that took years to recover from. The ultimate result was a complete shift in the nature of the ECAC and a further tipping in the balance of power among Eastern schools.

Partly because of the weakened schedule and partly because of Cornell's own improvement, the 1984–85 version of the Big Red made a leap from 11 wins to 18 wins, and Cornell suddenly stepped back into the ECAC tournament after a three-year absence. Behind the leadership of defenseman Mike Schafer and the exploits of freshman Joe Nieuwendyk, Cornell rode a renewed enthusiasm back to Boston Garden after blitzing Yale in the first playoff games at Lynah Rink in four years. Cornell's run ended in the ECAC semifinals with a loss to eventual NCAA champion Rensselaer.

The next season would bring even bigger thrills. Early in 1985–86, Yale defeated Cornell at Lynah Rink in overtime, as future NHL forward Randy Wood potted a hat trick.

But the overtime fun was just beginning.

The Big Red recovered at just the right time, winning three straight, including two in overtime, then coming home to win an ECAC quarterfinal series with Vermont. And once again, the fans sent the Big Red off to Boston with an on-ice celebration.

Once at Boston Garden, the Big Red hooked up with Yale again, and this time one overtime was not enough. "The Cardiac Kids" from Cornell, having already played nine overtime games during the season, rode the back of sophomore goaltender Doug Dadswell to defeat the Bulldogs 3-2 on a goal by Duanne Moeser. Dadswell had 59 saves as he single-handedly shut down the potent Yale offense with a goaltending performance unseen from a Big Red goalie since Ken Dryden.

In the ECAC finals, the Big Red met up with Clarkson, which just had a big upset of its own by knocking off a Harvard team on its way to the Frozen Four. And just for good measure, the Big Red sent this one to overtime too. Cornell built a 2-0 lead only to see Clarkson tie it on two power-play goals in the second period. After a scoreless third, Cornell freshman Chris Grenier scored the game-winner, and Dadswell had 33 more saves, giving the Big Red its first title in six years and its first NCAA berth in five.

Still playing under the two-game, total-goal format, Cornell dropped the first game at Denver 4-2. In Game 2, Cornell jumped out with three goals in a 1:45 span, including two by Nieuwendyk, and briefly held the total-goal series lead. But Cornell was unable to sustain the edge, winning the game but losing the series.

The departure of leaders like Schafer and Pete Natyshak left a definite void in 1986–87. Despite Nieuwendyk's heroics, which included hat tricks in his final two games, the Big Red mustered just 11 wins and missed the playoffs again. In addition, the Big Red was beset by discipline problems, both on and off the ice.

After just five seasons, Lou Reycroft was gone, the shortest stint of any Cornell coach in the modern era. He went on to be a successful chief amateur scout for the New Jersey Devils, serving under an old Cornell nemesis, former Providence coach Lou Lamoriello.

Cornell's Jeff Baikie scores against Brown in a 7-2 win on March 2, 1981. Baikie was the Big Red's leading scorer in 1982–83 as Cornell won the Ivy League crown. The team's record was mediocre, however, and it failed to make the ECAC playoffs for the second straight season. (*Cornell Daily Sun.*)

Darren Eliot, receiving the Nicky Bawlf Award as team MVP from Cornell athletic director Mike Slive, was a bright spot in the 1982–83 season, garnering all-America honors. Cornell won its last four games of the season to finish 13-10-3. Eliot went on to play for Canada's 1984 Olympic team. (Cornell Athletic Communications.)

Duanne Moeser, Cornell's leading scorer his sophomore year, accepts the 1983–84 team MVP award. He scored a total of 81 goals and 177 points in his four-year career. Despite a disappointing season in 1982–83, the Big Red featured a prominent freshman class that was destined for later success, including future captains Moeser, Pete Natyshak, and Mike Schafer. The Big Red won another Ivy League title, but failed to make the ECAC playoffs for the third consecutive season. (Cornell Athletic Communications.)

With the departure of six ECAC schools to form Hockey East, Cornell lost rivalries with the likes of Boston University and Providence. This also left Harvard as the dominant ECAC team. Here, in one of the highlights of the 1984–85 season, Dave Shippel scores the game-winning goal in overtime at Harvard, giving Cornell its 10th straight win. It would be more than 10 years before Cornell would defeat Harvard again in the regular season. (*Cornell Daily Sun.*)

Lou Reycroft recruited an outstanding class for the 1984–85 season, led by Joe Nieuwendyk, who burst onto the Cornell scene, displaying his offensive gifts immediately. Nieuwendyk recorded 21 goals and was named the ECAC Rookie of the Year, the first such honor for a Cornell player since Doug Ferguson 20 years earlier. This recruiting class, which also included Chris Norton and Doug Dadswell—immediately inserted as the team's No. 1 goaltender— helped the team regain its winning form in going 18-10-2. That was aided, in part, by a reformulated ECAC, following the departure of six schools that had left to create Hockey East. As a result, Cornell finished fourth in the ECAC and hosted a first-round playoff series, defeating high-powered Yale in two games. The Big Red went on to lose the ECAC semifinals 5-1 to a Rensselaer team on its way to a national championship. (Cornell Athletic Communications/Jon Crispin.)

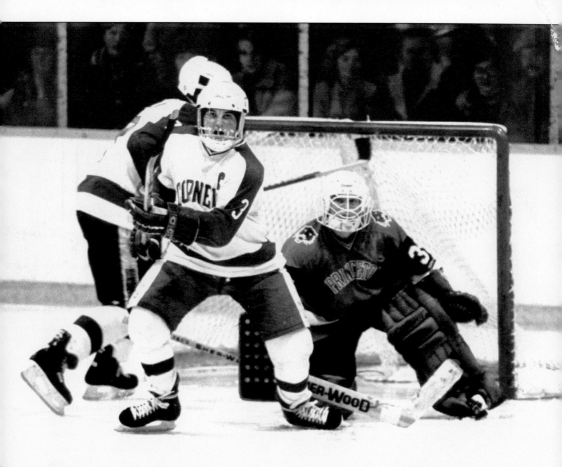

Reycroft often put Mike Schafer up front on the power play. Schafer's fiery tenacity and willingness to do what it took to win endeared him to the Faithful. His spirit was most on display in a famous incident in the 1983–84 season, when Schafer broke a stick over his head as he was called during introductions before a Harvard game. Legend has it, the stick was partially broken beforehand. Nevertheless, Lynah roared its approval. The Big Red fell behind 4-0 in the game but rallied, only to have Schafer score the eventual game-winner. "Kill, Schafer, Kill" became a popular refrain. But Schafer was more than a showman; he was a true team leader, and unquestionably future coaching material. (Cornell Athletic Communications/Jon Crispin.)

A new tradition was born at Lynah Rink when fans, excited to see the Big Red going back to the Boston Garden, spontaneously jumped the boards to congratulate the players on the ice following the Big Red's first-round ECAC playoff sweep of Yale in 1985. Here, a similar celebration follows the 1986 first-round series win over Vermont. (Cornell Athletic Communications/Jon Crispin.)

Chris Norton does what he can to clear the puck. Norton, the backbone of a team that had been depleted through the graduation and departure of several stars, was a captain in 1987–88 when Cornell transitioned to a new coach. An 11th-round NHL draft pick, Norton graduated as one of the top-scoring defensemen in Big Red history with 118 points. (*Ithaca Journal.*)

Doug Dadswell entered Cornell in 1984, winning the starting goaltender's job and playing in almost every game for two seasons. Dadswell was the rock on the 1985–86 team, whose players became known as "the Cardiac Kids," playing nine overtime games during the regular season, four of which were wins. Two of those came on the ECAC's final weekend, road wins at Vermont and Rensselaer that gave the Big Red a home-ice spot in the playoffs. After disposing of Vermont, Cornell went to the Garden, where the Cardiac Kids were in full display and Dadswell was dazzling. In the ECAC semifinals, Dadswell stopped 57 shots, often in spectacular fashion, as Cornell defeated Yale in double overtime. The next day, in Cornell's 11th overtime game of the season, freshman Chris Grenier's goal gave the Big Red the ECAC tournament championship. Dadswell left after the season, forgoing his final two years at Cornell to turn professional. His brief NHL career consisted of 28 games with Calgary, but he left with an ECAC tournament MVP trophy under his belt. (Tim McKinney.)

Pete Natyshak celebrates as Cornell wins the 1986 ECAC tournament on a goal by freshman Chris Grenier in overtime. Cornell went on to lose a total-goal NCAA series to Denver but, at 21-7-4, the Big Red had its first 20-win season in seven years. (Cornell Athletic Communications.)

Joe Nieuwendyk shreds the Colgate defense and scores again. Despite Nieuwendyk's second straight all-America performance, the 1986–87 team tumbled into ninth place in the ECAC and missed the playoffs. Nieuwendyk capped his career with hat tricks in his final two games, then left to join the NHL's Calgary Flames. (Charles Harrington.)

Lou Reycroft advises Mark Major (16) and Pete Marcov (19). Reycroft and Cornell parted ways following the 1986–87 season. (Cornell Athletic Communications/Jonathan K. Barkey.)

Six

BRIAN MCCUTCHEON
UPS AND DOWNS

After the departure of coach Lou Reycroft, Cornell turned to former Big Red captain Brian McCutcheon to get the program back on solid footing. After leaving Cornell as a student, McCutcheon's professional playing career included a stint in the NHL with Detroit. He then went on to coaching, and enjoyed a successful tenure at Division III Elmira before returning to his alma mater.

McCutcheon's first group was led by senior defenseman and captain Chris Norton and featured two freshman goaltenders—Corrie D'Alessio and Jim Crozier. The Big Red cruised to an 18-6 record, and things looked great. That is, until some ominous signs developed. The Big Red lost its last game of the regular season at Vermont, then lost Game 1 of the ECAC quarterfinal playoff series to Clarkson. The defeat was only the second home playoff loss in Cornell history. The Big Red won Game 2, but lost the mini-game that followed, and the season was over.

The next two seasons featured 16 wins each and a frustrating series of ups and downs. In 1989–90, the Big Red was in contention for an ECAC title until a 5-2 loss at Harvard marked another omen. It was Harvard's 11th straight win over Cornell, including all seven meetings since McCutcheon had taken over. So it figures that, after dropping the last two games of the regular season, the Big Red was left to face Harvard in the ECAC playoffs.

But the Cornell players mustered the will to defeat their rivals, in what turned out to be the only two wins against Harvard during the McCutcheon era. The series marked the end of Harvard coach Bill Cleary's career. Cleary said an emotional goodbye just outside the visiting locker room at Lynah Rink, as he retired from coaching to become Harvard's athletic director. Cornell advanced in the playoffs, only to again fall agonizingly short of an ECAC title.

Optimism was high for the 1990–91 season. Two straight strong recruiting classes, plus the now-senior class McCutcheon had inherited, had fallen together to create Cornell's most talented group in years. The Big Red lived up to the enthusiasm early on, coming out 4-0-2. That was before Cornell smacked into a cold, hard reality known as Harvard, and took an 8-3 beating—the 11th straight regular-season loss to the Crimson.

Undaunted, the Big Red reached an ECAC record of 13-2-2 and first place as Harvard came to town for the rematch in February. Less than a minute away from another loss, Cornell's Tim

Vanini's slapper found the net, tying the game 2-2, which is how it ended. It was not a win, but it was not a loss either. With four games to go, Cornell was sitting pretty.

Optimism sunk, however, when the Big Red lost three of the next four games, including the last two at home, and often in ugly fashion. Hopes of a regular-season title were erased.

With the second season, however, came renewed enthusiasm, especially after the Big Red demolished Colgate—one year removed from its trip to the NCAA finals—in two playoff games at Lynah. This propelled Cornell to Boston Garden, where the team met a tough St. Lawrence squad it had beaten twice in the regular season. Once again, however, Cornell came agonizingly close but missed the mark, as Dan Laperriere's overtime goal crushed the Big Red.

Cornell squeaked into the NCAA tournament, where it again tantalized fans with a dramatic Game 1 win at Michigan, only to lose the best-of-three series.

Despite the disappointments, the 1990–91 season marked the highlight of the McCutcheon era. Dan Ratushny and Kent Manderville left after that season for the Olympics and never returned. The strong senior class was gone, and Ryan Hughes was left to carry much of the offense himself.

Oddly, Cornell actually went farther in the ECAC tournament in 1991–92 than in any other year of that era. After a mediocre regular season, the Big Red won a playoff at Yale, pulled out a double-overtime thriller in the ECAC semifinals against Clarkson on a goal by Tyler McManus, then lost in the finals. Goalie Parris Duffus was named an all-American in 1991–92, but he then departed school early, leaving Cornell in a rare goaltending lurch that hastened the Big Red's demise.

In 1992–93, things reached their nadir. The recruiting failed to keep up with the personnel losses, and two straight crushing overtime defeats propelled the Big Red to an 11-game losing streak and elimination from ECAC playoff contention. Amidst it all, the Big Red faced NCAA sanctions after its booster housing program was deemed in violation of NCAA rules. Cornell got away with a slap on the wrist, and players were forced to pony up some cash, which was donated to a charity. But it was another chink in the armor for the once-mighty Big Red.

After two more years of being unable to get past the quarterfinal round, and a regular-season winless streak against Harvard that reached 20 games (2-16-1 overall in the era), McCutcheon was let go. He moved on to begin what would become a very successful career coaching professional hockey.

Former captain Brian McCutcheon returned to coach Cornell in 1987 after a successful stint as head coach at Division III Elmira College. (*Cornell Daily Sun.*)

McCutcheon inherited a strong recruiting class, which included Trent Andison (19), Doug Derraugh, Bruce Frauley, and Tim Vanini. Andison, a consistent four-year performer for the Big Red, started off by winning the 1987–88 ECAC Rookie of the Year Award. (William H. Kim.)

Peter Ciavaglia drives a shot past Big Red goalie Corrie D'Alessio during what became known as "the Boston Massacre," a 9-1 drubbing at Bright Arena at the hands of Harvard early in the 1988–89 season. Harvard was destined for a national championship, while Cornell went through a rebuilding year. (*Cornell Daily Sun.*)

Coach McCutcheon's early recruiting classes continued to be strong. In 1989–90, the Big Red brought in Kent Manderville and Ryan Hughes, both of whom would be second-round NHL draft choices. Manderville won the 1989–90 ECAC Rookie of the Year Award and played one more season before joining the Canadian Olympic team. He did not return to Cornell and instead embarked on a lengthy NHL career, mainly as a productive third-line checker.(Tim McKinney.)

Cornell forward Phil Nobel (center) celebrates after defeating Harvard in the first round of the 1990 ECAC tournament. Cornell swept the series in two games at Lynah Rink, marking the Big Red's only wins against the Crimson in an eight-year span. Cornell had limped into the playoffs after losing its last two games of the season. But hopes were renewed as the Big Red knocked off Harvard and returned to the Boston Garden. (*Cornell Daily Sun.*)

In the defining moment of the 1990 ECAC tournament semifinals against Rensselaer, Cornell forward Ross Lemon (right) is taken down, leading to a penalty shot. Lemon, the team's leading scorer that season as a senior, was denied on the shot by Rensselaer goaltender Sean Kennedy, and RPI held on to win the game. It would be the first in a series of "close but no cigar" moments for the Big Red in Boston during this era. (*Cornell Daily Sun.*)

Mike Schafer waits in the wings. After graduating from Cornell, Schafer (standing, left) became an assistant coach for the Big Red, serving for three years under Brian McCutcheon (standing, right). Schafer then left to become an assistant at Western Michigan, where he expanded his reputation as a standout recruiter. (*Cornell Daily Sun*/Steve Kim.)

Casey Jones (foreground) was a 100-point scorer and a captain in his four-year career that ended in 1990. After graduation, he replaced Mike Schafer as assistant coach under Brian McCutcheon. Jones eventually landed as a top assistant at Ohio State, where he presided over four NCAA tournament teams. (*Cornell Daily Sun*/Jim Leynse.)

The 1990–91 ECAC season came to a bitter end for the Big Red when St. Lawrence defenseman Dan Laperriere dribbled one through traffic and past Cornell goalie Jim Crozier (above) in overtime of the semifinals. Cornell, playing with its most-talented team under Brian McCutcheon, was crushed by the loss, but still managed to squeak into the NCAA tournament. (*Cornell Daily Sun.*)

As the ECAC's era of high scoring began to wane, Cornell's Ryan Hughes (center) gave the individual performance of his career when he scored four goals against Boston College on January 29, 1991, at Lynah Rink. Unfortunately, those were the only goals Cornell scored in that game, as the team lost to the Eagles 5-4. No Cornell player has scored four goals in a game since. (*Cornell Daily Sun.*)

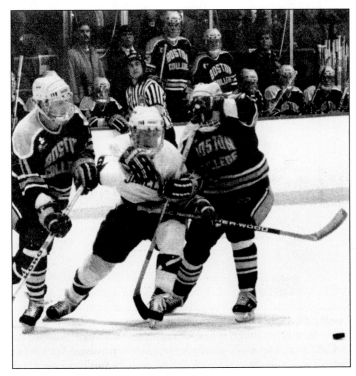

Dan Ratushny, a member of McCutcheon's first recruiting class, broke into the national spotlight during his sophomore season and achieved all-America honors. A dominant defenseman at both ends of the ice, Ratushny earned another all-America spot in 1990–91 before leaving to play for the Canadian Olympic team with teammate Kent Manderville. Neither returned to Cornell. Ratushny, whose sister Kim played on the Cornell women's team, went on to a professional career that included one NHL game for Vancouver. (Cornell Athletic Communications.)

Doug Derraugh, here battling Rensselaer's Joe Juneau, turned in a standout four-year career for the Big Red. Derraugh followed up his 16-goal junior season with a 30-goal campaign in 1990–91, making him the first Cornell player to reach that mark in 12 years. Derraugh teamed up with Trent Andison and Ryan Hughes to form the "HAD line," a play on their names and the fact that they *had* one goal per game. (*Cornell Daily Sun.*)

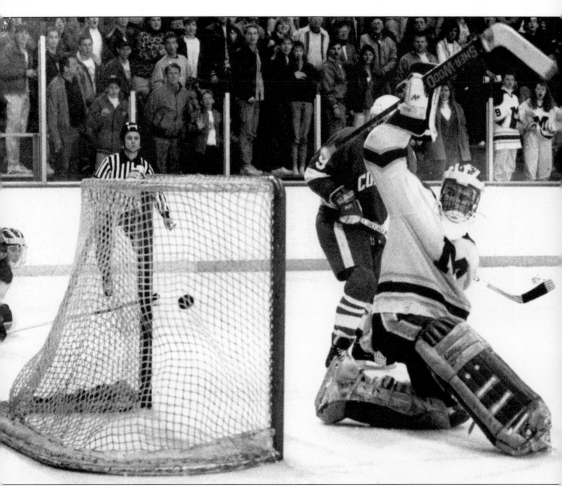

In Game 1 of the first-round NCAA series at Michigan, the Big Red stunned the home team when Kent Manderville tied the game with two seconds left, beating goalie Steve Shields (above). Trent Andison then won the game 21 seconds into overtime. Cornell lost the next two games, however, despite four goals from Doug Derraugh, and Michigan was on its way to becoming a national power. The series was also a watershed moment in the history of Michigan hockey, as a small but vocal group of Big Red fans "taught" the Yost Arena crowd how to perform. (*Cornell Daily Sun.*)

When two experienced senior goalies graduated after the 1990–91 season, Cornell was left with Parris Duffus, an unknown who had seen only limited action his freshman season. Duffus carried the Big Red to the 1992 ECAC championship game, and was named an all-American. He then left Cornell to begin a professional career, signing a contract to support his family. (*Cornell Daily Sun*/J. Eric Doctor.)

Some bare recruiting classes began to catch up to the Big Red. After missing the ECAC playoffs the year before, Cornell finished the 1993–94 season in eighth place in the ECAC at 8-17-5, and hosted a one-game play-in for the first time. An up-and-coming Princeton team took Cornell to overtime, but the Big Red's Geoff Lopatka (14) finished a hat trick for the game-winning goal. Cornell's season ended that weekend with a two-game sweep at the hands of Harvard. (*Cornell Daily Sun.*)

Seven

MIKE SCHAFER
THE REBIRTH OF A PROGRAM, PART II

Cornell hockey has had mostly ups but also a few downs in its long history since Lynah Rink was built. Few years were as disappointing as the three from 1992 to 1995, when Cornell finished 25-51-10. With that, the powers-that-be decided to change coaches, replacing one former captain with another, Mike Schafer, as coach.

The decision to change coaches came relatively late, in June, and Schafer was not hired until July 20, 1995. But when the choice was made, it was popular, since fans remembered the leadership of Schafer and the rest of the seniors in 1986 that held the team together on its way to an ECAC championship. Schafer also held the reputation of a strong recruiter as an assistant at Cornell. That reputation was enhanced by Schafer's work as an assistant at Western Michigan, where he helped build a team that made two NCAA tournaments, and by the perception that Cornell's recruiting had suffered after he left.

Schafer—who had previously given his blood, sweat, and tears for the Cornell program for eight years—could hardly contain his excitement upon returning: "When I left Cornell, I had mixed emotions because I loved the hockey program, and the Ithaca community meant a great deal to me. On the other hand, it was a tremendous opportunity to go work with coach Bill Wilkinson in a new environment. I felt that coaching in a different league would benefit my professional development. Being a head coach has always been a goal of mine and now it has become a reality. And it's even better—returning to a great university such as Cornell. It's like returning home."

Schafer came in with three goals: beat Harvard, get home ice for the ECAC tournament, and pack Lynah Rink. But his first job was to re-instill a sense of pride in the program, embracing everything that the Lynah Experience was all about and using it to his advantage. For example, Schafer had his players polish old trophies, study up on the program's history, and create new traditions that acknowledged the crowd's place in the scheme of things.

Beyond the intangibles, one of the most striking changes during the season was the immediate improvement in Cornell's special teams. After having ranked near the bottom for years, the Big Red was suddenly dominant on the power play and dangerous shorthanded.

The Big Red opened the ECAC schedule 4-0-2, though the team had its struggles out of conference, including big losses to Michigan State and Boston University, and a dubious loss at

Army. But the Big Red machine got rolling in the second half and went 11-1 heading into the playoffs. Two of Schafer's goals had already been reached: his team had beaten Harvard twice, and Cornell had earned home ice in the playoffs. In hosting Colgate, the Big Red reached goal No. 3: Lynah was packed and loud.

The last time Cornell had hosted a quarterfinal series in the ECAC tournament was five years earlier, also against Colgate. In that series, the Big Red had dominated in every way possible, pummeling the Red Raiders by a combined score of 18-4. No one was counting on that, however. People were just happy the Big Red had a home playoff series again, coming off three dark years.

Before the series, Schafer showed his players a tape of the on-ice celebration that had occurred after Cornell's playoff series win during his senior year in 1986. After viewing the video, forward Jamie Papp said, "I think everybody's adrenaline started flowing tenfold."

It showed. Cornell blitzed a very solid Colgate team from start to finish that weekend. Colgate was hit with grit, skill, stifling defense, and 8-3 and 8-1 losses. The crowd ate it up. Colgate coach (and former Cornell assistant) Don Vaughan said home crowds were usually good for a goal or two, but "this crowd had to be good for three or four. I've never seen Lynah Rink like this and I've seen a lot of games here."

A week later, Cornell defeated its archrival Harvard once again, this time for the ECAC tournament championship. An NCAA berth awaited, where Cornell fell agonizingly short to Lake Superior State.

But in Lake Placid, the crowd said it all: "Thank you Schafer!"

Cornell hockey was back.

In a tip of the hat to the Lynah Faithful, Mike Schafer started the tradition of players staying on the ice following each home game to salute the fans. (Ned Dykes.)

Endurance quickly became a trademark of Cornell teams under Mike Schafer, as the program embraced the efforts of new strength and conditioning coach Tom Howley. (Tim McKinney.)

Jason Elliott was an unknown quantity in 1995–96. But as Cornell marched to a huge stretch run, Elliott emerged as the No. 1 goalie. Before he was done, he had made history with back-to-back ECAC MVP awards. Although game programs listed that Elliott was from Australia, he had actually grown up in and played junior hockey in Canada. (Tim McKinney.)

Brad Chartrand beats Colgate goalie Dan Brenzavich during the 1996 ECAC playoffs at Lynah Rink. Cornell played well down the stretch, but no one expected the pure dominance exhibited in the two-game sweep. For Chartrand, it was a highlight in a breakout senior year, when he went from three-year role player to star, before forging an NHL career. (*Cornell Daily Sun.*)

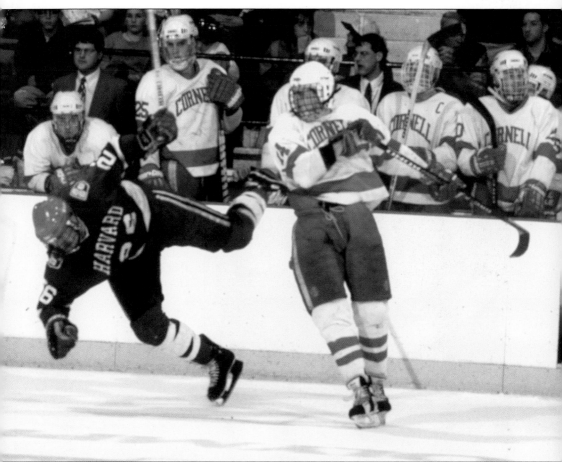

The 1996 ECAC championship match between Cornell and Harvard was the first all-Ivy ECAC tournament final since Cornell-Dartmouth in 1980 and the first between the Big Red and the Crimson since 1969. Harvard struck quickly, scoring in the game's first minute to stun Cornell, but the Big Red got physical and slammed the door from there. Matt Cooney and Mike Sancimino scored, and Cornell held Harvard to three shots in the third period to seal a 2-1 victory for the Big Red. Jason Elliott was named tournament MVP. After 10 years of waiting—its longest drought in ECAC tournament history—Cornell finally had another championship. (Nancie Battaglia.)

Mike Sancimino (right) battles Lake Superior State's Ted Laviolette during the 1996 NCAAs in Albany. Two early bad goals put Cornell in a hole, but the team eventually stormed back, overcoming a shorthanded goal and a disallowed goal of its own to tie the game at 4-4. But Lake Superior's Matt Alvey then scored the go-ahead goal, giving his team a 5-4 lead. The Big Red poured it on in the final minutes but came up short in the end. Cornell's best scoring chance came when P. C. Drouin ripped a slapper off the crossbar, a clang that still reverberates today. (*Ithaca Journal.*)

A two-time First Team All-ECAC performer, Steve Wilson played a pivotal role in Cornell's first back-to-back ECAC tournament championships in 27 years (1996 and 1997). (*Cornell Daily Sun.*)

Goaltender Jason Elliott stops future NHL forward Todd White on a breakaway to preserve Cornell's shutout against Clarkson in the 1997 ECAC championship game. Elliott was named tournament MVP for the second straight season. In the NCAAs, Cornell overcame Miami University in the third period to advance in the tournament for the first time in 25 years. The Big Red lost 6-2 to eventual champion North Dakota the next day. (Nancie Battaglia.)

This became a common sight during the Mike Schafer era—fans streaming onto the ice to celebrate a playoff series victory with the players—with Cornell hosting and winning a first-round ECAC playoff series in six of Schafer's first eight years as coach. The scene here, in 2000, was perhaps the most emotional, as captain Doug Stienstra is lifted by fans after the Big Red defeated rival Harvard in a two-game sweep. (Tim McKinney.)

All-American Matt Underhill came to Cornell and picked up where Jason Elliott had left off in goal. (Cornell Athletic Communications.)

Once a fierce Cornell rival, Boston University came to Lynah Rink for the first time in 20 years in November 2002. It was a much-anticipated match-up that gave Cornell a chance to test itself against major national competition. The Big Red came through with flying colors, dominating the Terriers in two games, and prompting legendary BU coach Jack Parker (second from right) to proclaim, "It was like men against boys." (Adriano Manocchia.)

For three straight years, Cornell came up just short of its 10th ECAC title, including a 2002 overtime loss to rival Harvard. But while facing another defeat to Harvard in 2003, Ryan Vesce won a face-off back to Mark McRae (foreground), who found a seam through which to shoot. McRae's slapper found the back of the net with 33 seconds left, sending the game to overtime. (Jeff Wang.)

The Crimson killer strikes again. Sam Paolini (left), well known for his huge games against Harvard, saved his best for last. Paolini's slapper from the left wing beat Harvard goalie Dov Grumet-Morris to give Cornell a dramatic 4-3 overtime win, its elusive 10th ECAC tournament championship, and a No. 1 overall seed in the NCAA tournament. (Jeff Wang.)

Cornell fell behind 3-0 to New Hampshire in the 2003 Frozen Four semifinals, before the Big Red started a comeback with this Ryan Vesce power-play goal. It was the last power-play goal scored by the dominant five-man unit that had spent the better part of three seasons playing together. The group included Vesce and four seniors—Mark McRae, Sam Paolini, Doug Murray, and Stephen Bâby. (Pedro Cancel.)

At six-foot-three and 240 pounds, Doug Murray was a menacing presence on the Cornell back-line for four years and a key component of the Big Red's NCAA tournament teams in 2002 and 2003. The first Cornell player from Sweden, Murray developed into one of the college hockey's best defensemen, with a rocket shot, crushing checking, unmatched strength, and pinpoint positioning. In 2002, Murray became Cornell's first Hobey Baker Award finalist in 15 years. (Pedro Cancel.)

It became obvious early in his freshman year that Dave LeNeveu was special, even among the historically strong legacy of Cornell goaltenders. During his sophomore year, playing nearly every minute in net—except the four games he missed while participating in the World Junior Championships—LeNeveu rewrote history, breaking a 50-year NCAA record for goals-against average and the Cornell single-season shutout mark. He was a Hobey Baker Award runner-up before declaring his intentions to go professional. (Pedro Cancel.)

Stephen Bâby (21), at six-foot-five and 235 pounds, epitomized Cornell hockey at the turn of the millennium. He used his size to dominate the boards and wear down opponents. (Pedro Cancel.)

Cornell rallied frantically in the final minutes of the 2003 Frozen Four semifinal against New Hampshire, but the Big Red missed its best opportunity to tie when Wildcats goalie Mike Ayers lunged across the crease and stopped a Stephen Bâby shot (above) with his helmet. (Adriano Manocchia.)

From Sarnia, Ontario, Cam (left) and Chris Abbott became the fifth set of twins to suit up for the Big Red when they arrived in 2002, joining past tandems the Fergusons, Webers, Geigers, and McRaes. (Ned Dykes.)

In November 2003, Mark McCutcheon (right) became the first legacy player to dress for a varsity game in Cornell history, joining his dad, Brian (left), who was a team captain in 1971 and the Big Red head coach for eight years. (*Cornell Daily Sun*/Ned Dykes.)

Class of 1972 Cornell hockey alumnus Craig Brush (left) bought a minor-league hockey franchise in Florida and soon started one of the premier Christmastime college hockey tournaments, the Florida Everblades Classic. Cornell, a perennial competitor, did not win the tournament until its fourth year, in 2003, when Greg Hornby beat Ohio State in overtime. The tournament MVP was Mike Iggulden (right), who accepted his trophy from Brush. (Ned Dykes.)

The first Cornell player from Texas, David McKee had some big shoes to fill when he came to Ithaca in 2003. Replacing all-American Dave LeNeveu, McKee won the ECAC Rookie of the Year Award while starting every game for the Big Red during his freshman season. (Ned Dykes.)

Eight

THE LYNAH EXPERIENCE
COME ALL YE FAITHFUL

Lynah Rink. Just saying the name invokes strong emotions in Cornell hockey fans, all of them positive.

Hockey is a sport best seen live. It is said that if a non-believer sees a game live, he will be hooked for life. Nowhere is this more apparent than at Lynah.

It might not look like much when there is no game being played—just an old brick building with low-hanging lights, wooden rafters, and an open west side with a brick wall. But in this day and age of state-of-the-art, modern facilities, one would be hard-pressed to find another hockey building on the planet with the amount of history that is soaked into this arena's pores.

Lynah Rink transcends the game itself. It is as much a part of the game as the actual game. For the Lynah Faithful, the complete experience is one that grips fans from the beginning of the season straight through to its climactic moments.

"You hear about it, but you figure other coaches from other schools are saying the same thing," said former Big Red captain Stephen Bâby. "Then you come out here and see it, and you say 'Wow! This is unbelievable.' And then you play your first game, and it's even 10 times greater than that, and you didn't think it could be better than when you were sitting in the stands on your recruiting trip, but somehow it is."

It begins well before the season, with the famed "Ticket Line," a constantly shifting, always frustrating, but ultimately memorable process.

When the season comes, each game is met with a crescendo of anticipation.

Until the early 1970s, people squeezed into Lynah Rink in greater numbers than the 3,826 it holds today. A popular refrain from public-address announcer Barlow Ware was, "Please move to the center of the section so that more people can sit." As many as 4,500 people sometimes shoe-horned their way in, until fire marshals put an end to that, requiring that seats be numbered and each person be assigned a spot.

Games once began at 8 p.m., then 7:30, then 7 p.m. In the "good old days," fans would arrive hours early, creating a festive atmosphere. Now, with advance sales of most every ticket, fans no longer have to queue up hours in advance to find a good seat. It also means many fans choose to come just before, or after, face-off.

The game itself proceeds. The Faithful do not just follow along, but become part of the event. The pep band and the crowd interact, not as separate parts competing for attention, but as a unit in a well-organized, organic choral experience. Well-timed chants and songs are passed down over the years, always evolving, with new ones added and others deleted.

There is always debate. Is the crowd too unruly? Is the crowd too sedate? Do the new students understand the tradition? Which chants are appropriate in the repertoire and which are not? Lest anyone thinks this is a new phenomenon, it was noted in 1962: "It is regrettable that the Cornell crowd is getting a bad reputation for being so unruly. . . . Officials hate to work here. The spectators are too close to the rink. They should enclose it or something; they should at least enclose the penalty box area, even if it's chicken wire."

Of course, that was the same year that Lynah Rink established itself as the place to be. The *Cornellian* noted the achievement, first stating that typically at Cornell sporting events, "the noise generated from the small section seating the visiting school's faithful drowns out the half-hearted uninspired drones of Cornellians." But it was different now. "There *is* such a thing as school spirit after all. This is Cornell hockey."

In a day when so many other historic arenas have been replaced, Lynah Rink still stands. Wrigley Field may be a little more corporate, Fenway Park may have luxury boxes. So too may Lynah Rink someday be "upgraded" to accommodate more modern necessities. Nevertheless, like the aforementioned ballparks, Lynah Rink remains as a living, breathing monument.

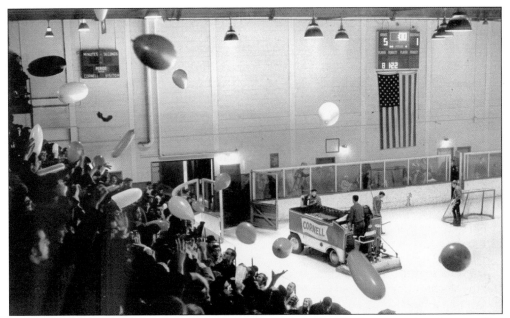

Balloons twirl between periods at Lynah Rink as a *c.* 1970 Zamboni remakes the ice. The balloons were a tradition at Lynah for a while, particularly as a way to pass time while waiting for the game to start. Because seats were not reserved then, people would show up hours before the first face-off and file in at 6:30, ninety minutes before the common start time of the era. (Cornell University Archives.)

The scarcity and popularity of tickets to Cornell games at Lynah Rink gave birth to the Ticket Line. Under current formalities, it's unlikely we will ever again see someone sleeping in Barton Hall under a pyramid of beer cans. (Cornell University Archives/Russell C. Hamilton.)

Kevin Kramer (left) and Alan Rosenthal celebrate their place in the Ticket Line before the 1970–71 season. Each year since the 1960s, students have gone through the line to land season tickets to Lynah Rink. Originally, one had to stay in line for several nights in Barton Hall while waiting for the tickets to go on sale. The procedure for ticket sales has undergone almost annual modification, as Cornell tries to find a system that is safe and fair, limits missed classroom time, and rewards the most rabid fans. (Cornell University Archives/Russell Hamilton.)

The original cowbell used by Neil Cohen from 1968 to 1972 (above) was struck with the handle of a knife that was wrapped with tape at its sharp end so it could be held. Cohen took a basic Latin rhythm his high school band had used and brought it to Lynah Rink. The rhythm is banged out on the bell, followed by a cheer of "Fight" from the crowd, then repeated a second time—a Cornell hockey staple. (Neil Cohen.)

When Neil Cohen graduated in 1972, he had no idea he had started a tradition that would carry on for decades, passed down from performer to performer. At times there have been twin cowbells, as during the late 1980s, when Dr. John Comisi played (far right). For a couple of years, there was even a cowbell band, complete with washboard and wood block supplying rhythm. At left, Adriano Manocchia bangs the bell at Princeton's Baker Rink in 2003. (*Cornell Daily Sun*/Ned Dykes.)

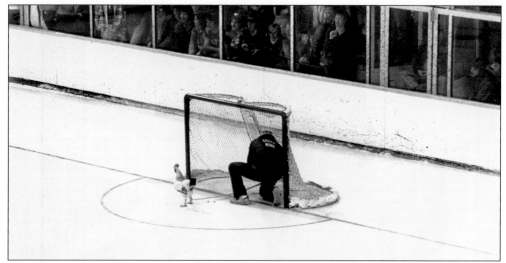

One of the more famous (or infamous) Lynah traditions—tossing fish on the ice prior to the start of home games against Harvard—began in the early 1970s. Years ago, when Harvard fans mocked Cornell's agriculture school by tying a live chicken to Cornell's goalpost (above), the Faithful eventually responded in kind. But after several fowl perished in the line of duty, the fans turned to tossing fish, mocking Harvard's proximity to Boston Harbor. (Cornell University Archives/Sol Goldberg.)

Often-perplexed Harvard players wait for the ice to be cleaned after the annual bombardment of fish (or facsimiles thereof). (Adriano Manocchia.)

The Cornell Big Red Pep Band is not only a big part of the Lynah mystique but also frequently travels to support the team on the road. Here, the band performs in Princeton's Baker Rink. (Ned Dykes.)

The Lynah Faithful have always found ways to get under the skin of visiting players, but it was easier to do when the glass was low and the student section stretched unbroken halfway around the rink. Eventually, however, Section C got plastic seats and became a booster section, splitting the student fans, and rink renovations in 2000 increased the height of the glass around the boards. (*Cornell Daily Sun.*)

Concerned about complaints that the fans' cheers had become, at times, too vulgar, Mike Schafer, in his inaugural season as head coach in 1995, asked the Lynah crowd to eliminate the vulgarity while maintaining the enthusiasm and support. Though the struggle over where to draw the line between spirit and rudeness goes back to Lynah's early days, the Faithful by and large have cooperated when asked to do so. (*Cornell Daily Sun.*)

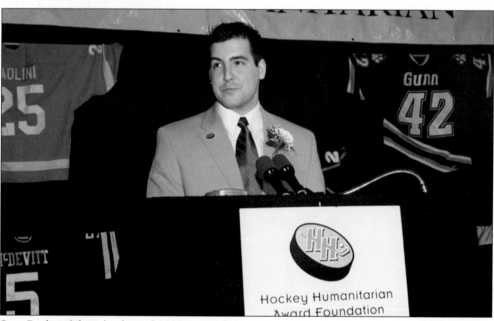

Sam Paolini (above), class of 2003, started the "Power Play for Prevention" program to raise funds for the Ithaca Breast Cancer Alliance, and set up several other community service initiatives as well. He was honored with the national Hockey Humanitarian Award in 2003. Though Paolini is the most shining example, Cornell players have consistently given back to the community that passionately supports them.

Dave Nulle's flamboyant costumes are a staple when he drives the Zamboni between periods of each Cornell home game. The Zamboni was once driven by Gene Beavers and, before that, Lou Mobbs, who in earlier days used to plow snow off Beebe Lake with a horse-drawn scraper and shovel. The original Zamboni, delivered to Lynah Rink by Frank Zamboni himself in 1956, was used until 1981. (Ned Dykes.)

Once a regular occurrence, complete with a "his" and "hers" striptease act at the last home game of each season, the Cornell Bear performance has been phased out of the between-periods festivities at Lynah. (Charles Harrington.)

Mike Teeter began working as goal judge in 1962 and remained in his seat well into the 21st century. He became a close friend of Ned Harkness and an inspiration to many generations of hockey players. Traveling with the team as the equipment manager, Teeter became one of Cornell Hockey's most beloved figures.

Grady Whittenburg (left) called Cornell games for 12 seasons (1990–2002). Sam Woodside (far right), the original "Voice of the Big Red," was on the microphone for both of Cornell's national championships. Calling hockey sticks "shillelaghs," describing penalized players as "going to jail," and sometimes referring to the puck as a "ball," Woodside conveyed the glory years of Cornell hockey to thousands of fans who could not attend the games. (Binghamton Senators/Cornell University Archives.)

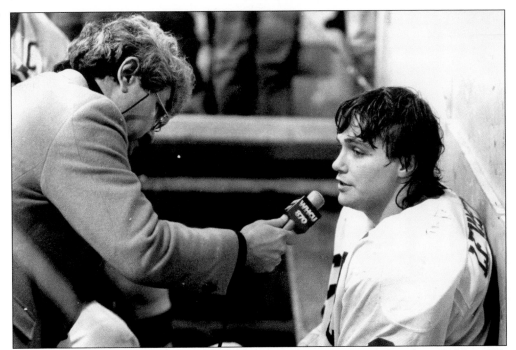

Roy Ives (left) interviews Rob Levasseur after the player's final game at Lynah, on February 25, 1989. Ives described Cornell hockey on WHCU with his sidekick, Tom Joseph, through most of the 1970s. After a less-than-satisfactory sojourn to professional hockey, Ives returned to Ithaca as Cornell's radio voice again until 1990. (*Cornell Daily Sun*/Troy Norin.)

Ozzie Richardson sat right next to the Cornell bench and became a familiar part of the cast of characters at Lynah Rink in the 1960s and 1970s. If an official dawdled in the face-off circle after a play stoppage, Ozzie would bellow, "Drop the puck, turkey!" in a voice that reverberated throughout the building. He often leaned over the glass to give unsuspecting officials a blast from his air horn as they skated past. (*Ithaca Journal*.)

Fans in the student sections at Lynah, feigning boredom, hold up sections of the *Cornell Daily Sun* while the visiting team is introduced. Afterward, the papers are wadded up and chucked on the ice, where awaiting rink staff faithfully clean up the debris. According to Jeff Hopkins, class of 1982, he stole the idea from University of Scranton basketball fans. "It seemed a natural fit for introductions, since that was the only time you could do it without missing part of the game." (*Cornell Daily Sun*.)

"It's all your fault!" Lynah fans explain to an opposing goaltender the reason that Cornell has just scored a goal. Few crowds can heckle goaltenders with the *joie de vivre* of the Lynah Faithful. (Ned Dykes.)

"Good evening, hockey fans." In Lynah Rink's first 45 years, only two men served as permanent public-address announcers—Barlow Ware (left) and Arthur Mintz. Ware held the job from the rink's opening until 1986, when he broke his leg in an automobile accident. Bob Julian, his backup, filled in until Mintz was named permanent replacement in 1987–88. Said Mintz, "Barlow invented 'Good evening hockey fans.' I restored it and have used it from the day I started."

A sampling of game programs through the years.

Long after becoming an NHL superstar, Joe Nieuwendyk kept close ties to the Ithaca area. He won the Stanley Cup on three occasions—in 1989 with Calgary, 1999 with Dallas, and 2003 with New Jersey—and after the latter two championships, Nieuwendyk brought the Cup back to Ithaca to celebrate. During Nieuwendyk's visit in 1999, Cornell held a reception at Moakley House for fans, and in 2003, the Cup was the centerpiece of a fund-raising effort at the annual summer alumni game for Mike Tallman, a former Cornell player who had been paralyzed in a hockey accident a few months earlier. Here, Nieuwendyk raises the cup with former teammate Mike Schafer at Dunbar's, a popular Ithaca watering hole.